THIS BOOK BELONGS TO:

CHRISTMAS 2002

Christmas with Southern Living® 2002

Edited by Rebecca Brennan,
Julie Gunter, and Lauren Brooks

Oxmoor House®

Book Division of Southern Progress Corporation
P. O. Box 2463, Birmingham, Alabama 35201

ISBN: 0-8487-2522-0
ISSN: 0747-7791
Printed in the United States of America
First Printing 2002

Christmas with Southern Living® 2002
Editor: Rebecca Brennan
Foods Editor: Julie Gunter
Associate Editor: Lauren Caswell Brooks
Editorial Assistant: Suzanne Powell
Senior Designer: Melissa M. Clark
Senior Photographer: Jim Bathie
Photographer: Brit Huckabay
Senior Photo Stylist: Kay E. Clarke
Photo Sylist: Ashley Wyatt
Illustrator: Kelly Davis
Director, Test Kitchens: Elizabeth Tyler Luckett
Assistant Director, Test Kitchens: Julie Christopher
Recipe Editor: Gayle Hays Sadler
Test Kitchens Staff: Jennifer A. Cofield; Gretchen P. Feldtman, R.D.; David Gallent; Ana Price Kelly; Kathleen Royal Phillips; Jan A. Smith
Publishing Systems Administrator: Rick Tucker
Director, Production and Distribution: Phillip Lee
Books Production Manager: Theresa L. Beste
Production Assistant: Faye Porter Bonner

Contributors
Copy Editor: Adrienne Short Davis
Editorial Interns: Megan Graves, McCharen Pratt
Stylist Assistants: Lauren Brasher, Cathy Mathews

Front cover: Bourbon-Chocolate Pecan Pie, page 143
Back cover, clockwise from top left: All Aglow, page 123; Abundantly Appealing, page 39; Toile Santa, page 170; Mocha-Orange Bûche de Noël, page 88

CONTENTS

WITH SOUTHERN STYLE
8

TABLETOP MAGIC
30

CASUAL HOLIDAY MEALS
48

THERE'S NO PLACE LIKE HOME
94

IT'S THE THOUGHT
126

HOLIDAY RECIPES
138

Where to Find It, 170

Patterns & Instructions, 172

Index, 173

Contributors, 176

Holiday Planning Guide, 177

WITH SOUTHERN STYLE

Renowned for hospitality, the South is especially welcoming at Christmastime with homes resplendently attired in native greenery and natural materials.

ENCHANTING ENTRIES

Wreaths and garlands set the standard for outdoor decorating, but this year add a new twist. For example, the garland pictured here is decked out with eucalyptus branches and trimmed with twig balls, pinecones, and ribbons. Turn the page for more fresh ideas.

1 A brick facade poses no problem for hanging a garland. Using a hammer, tap masonry nails into place in the mortar part of the brickwork. Leave plenty of nail showing to allow space for the garland to hang.

2 Once the nails are in place, drape the garland over the doorway. We used two garlands to give more visual weight. For additional fullness, tuck in or wire greenery clippings to the garland.

3 Pinecones are inexpensive embellishments for garlands and wreaths. Wrap floral wire around the bottom of the cone, between the rows of petals. Twist the wire to secure, and use the ends to attach the pinecone to the garland or wreath. Use wire to attach the twig balls, as well.

4 Holiday decorating calls for loads of ribbons and bows. For a quick-and-easy bow, from a long length of ribbon, form a few big loops then twist floral wire tightly around the center. Make lots of loops for a big bow. Pull the loops toward the center to fluff the bow. Attach the bow to the garland using the wire ends.

Magnolia Magnificence

▲ Steeped in Southern lore, magnolia is the region's quintessential holiday greenery. The wreath shown uses the versatile leaf to full advantage, contrasting the glossy green top side with the rich brown of the underside. Sprigs of feathery juniper add a lacy complement. Two metal mesh cones wired to the wreath are filled with fresh flowers and holly. A variety of decorative cones can be found at import and crafts stores.

Each peak of the swagged magnolia garland is punctuated with a flower-filled cone. Filling the cones with water-soaked floral foam in heavy-duty plastic bags keeps the flowers and greenery fresh for up to a week. ▶

Metal mesh cones and ribbons are attached to the garland using floral wire. ▼

PLAIN TO FANCY

Take one evergreen wreath and add embellishments to your heart's content. We show you how to go from plain to fancy in a few easy steps.

▲ Red ribbons on a green wreath convey the essence of Christmas decoration. If you're a purist, you may prefer to stop here with your add-ons. For the ribbons featured on this wreath, make a loop with a length of ribbon, twist a short floral wire around the loop, leaving ribbon ends free. Use the wire ends to attach the loops and a bow to the wreath.

▲ For a showier wreath, make a gathering foray into your backyard. Clusters of red berries display bright color, while dried hydrangea blooms, misted with red spray paint, contribute a delicate texture to the wreath. Long pieces of grapevine and twisted strands of dried grass convey a bountiful look. A lively plaid bow nestles behind the red one.

For sparkle, red and green Christmas ornaments and a glittery gold bow are added to the wreath. Long pieces of floral wire work well to attach all the decorations. ▶

Fresh and Fragrant

The heady aroma of evergreens, herbs, and florals instantly evokes thoughts of Christmas in these homes' holiday decorations. Backyard clippings and pots of favorite seasonal plants make it easy to blend natural materials with holiday finery for beautifully vibrant displays.

First Impressions

If space allows, consider placing your tree in the foyer. You'll enjoy passing it as you go about your daily business in the house, and guests will be able to appreciate one of your most outstanding decorations as soon as they enter.

Splendidly Swagged

A Fraser fir garland is the starting point for a mantel treatment whose elaborate looks belie its easy execution. Clusters of pepperberries tucked in among the garland's branches, a small crèche, and family heirloom cone trees are the central focus of the design.

Vases filled with cypress, juniper, and pepperberries give symmetry to the arrangement. On the coffee table, a deep red vase filled with juniper berries continues the design and complements the vases on the mantel. Water in the vases will keep the clippings fresh for about two weeks. The berries in the garland may dry out and need to be replaced after a few days, or place the stems in water vials to keep them fresh for longer. Hide the vials under the garland.

◀ Aromatic Ambience

Moss-wrapped pots of lavender impart an unconventional twist to this evergreen garland embellished with pepper-berry sprays. Basketwork figures of Mary and Joseph stand at the center. A cozy fire in the fireplace will release the lavender's fragrance; however, the heat dries the natural materials. Water the lavender frequently and keep fresh pepperberries on hand to replace dried ones as needed. To be safe, always keep greenery and decorations well away from the fireplace opening.

▲ Simple Styling

A modest papier-mâché nativity scene surrounded by fresh plants and greenery animates this tabletop. Two ivy topiaries act as a lush backdrop for the figurines, and the mixed-greenery garland over the mirror elegantly frames the traditional setting. An advantage of using fresh potted plants such as ivy, rosemary, and lavender as a part of your seasonal decorations is that the plants can be enjoyed long after the holidays are over and may be called into service for the next holiday season.

A Grand Gathering

Rosemary topiaries and a concrete cherub flanked by metal reindeer form the foundation for this tabletop tableau. The grouping is enlivened with clippings of pine, Fraser fir, cypress, deciduous holly, and pepperberries. Greenery and berries wired to the low-hanging chandelier visually link the tabletop arrangement and lighting fixture for a strong overall impact. Look for rosemary topiaries at nurseries and home-and-garden centers beginning around Thanksgiving.

Everlasting Charm

Dried flowers and grasses are used in abundance on this tree (and can be reused year after year). Feathers and dried grass stems create a fanlike tree topper. The bow hides the floral wire that holds the stems in place. Other decorations include seed and berry balls and raffia-tied bouquets of dried grass tucked among the branches. Thick, dried flower garlands complement the tree's large size.

ECLECTIC MIX

Juxtaposing elegant silver cups and candleholders with rustic pottery jugs holding seeded eucalyptus and heather showcases favored collectibles in a refreshingly individual holiday style.

Dining Room Drama

◀ Crystalline trees and silver accents bring to mind a wintry forest scene along the length of this dining table. A mix of greenery clippings unifies the grouping. Votive candles and pepperberries provide sparkle and color. In the center of the table, a silver compote holds an arrangement of potted plants and flowers. A small, water-soaked block of floral foam in the center of the compote holds the flower blooms, while the plants, in tiny plastic pots, are tucked in around the floral foam. When using silver containers for this purpose, be sure to line the bowls with plastic or with waterproof liners before adding the plants. To protect the tabletop, place the arrangement on top of a table runner.

Elegant and Easy

▼A boxwood wreath punctuated with berries encircles an ornate silver candleholder. Grazing reindeer are a whimsical touch. To protect your table, place the wreath and candleholder on a clear glass plate.

▲ HOLIDAY SETTING

Poinsettias—still in their plastic pots—are tucked into iron plant stands in the corners of this cozy sitting room. Sheet moss lining the plant stand baskets hides the pots. Note how simple touches such as the garland over the windows, the wreath, the pillows, and the silver trees mesh together for a cozy seasonal ambience.

TABLE MATTERS ▶

Set your dining table with a season-long decoration. Here, the Christmas tree-design plates determine the theme, which is reinforced with the family's collection of twig and painted trees arranged as a centerpiece. Rosemary topiaries in terra-cotta pots are a fresh (and fragrant) component, while ornament candles contribute a sparkling, festive air.

◀ Over the Top

A large gathering basket, secured to the chimneypiece with hooks and wires, is overflowing with a wide variety of seasonal clippings. A block of water-soaked floral foam placed in a heavy-duty plastic bag sits inside the basket and keeps the greenery fresh for a week to ten days. Deciduous holly berries awaken the garland and the basket with cheery color.

Pretty in Red and Green ▼

A berry-laden holly wreath, held in place with floral wire, is a jolly accent to the evergreen garland. The play of green and red is repeated on every shelf with evergreen clippings and shiny apples, and is seen again in the basket holding a rosemary topiary encircled by apples. For maximum impact, repeat decorative elements. Here, for example, evergreens and berries, apples, candles, and nutcrackers combine to strengthen the Christmassy atmosphere.

TABLETOP MAGIC

What fun to cover every tabletop with holiday cheer! Here, we show ways to use ordinary materials for extraordinary seasonal centerpieces and table settings.

Tastefully Set

With an evergreen garland and charger there's no need for a conventional centerpiece. Soak the greenery overnight before arranging, and it will stay fresh and fragrant for three to five days.

Trim the Table

Clippings of cedar, pine, boxwood, holly, and hypericum berries are wired together to make this garland that is attached with corsage pins to the tablecloth. For easy assembly of the garland, make several small bundles of clippings, then wire the bundles together to achieve the desired length for the garland.

Dressed for Dinner

Encircling your dinner plates with fresh greenery chargers is a quick and inexpensive way to a stunning table setting. Since the greenery stays fresh for several days, the chargers can be a fragrant part of your dining room decorations.

To make the charger, hot-glue sprigs of greenery and berries around the edges of a cardboard cake round (check with the grocery store bakery for these). We spray-painted ours, but it's okay to leave it unpainted, as well. You may prefer to remove the charger when dining.

Merry and Bright

Setting your table with Christmas china brings cheer to every meal. The table pictured here features plates with matching cups, chargers, flatware, place mats—even candles! However, you don't have to buy a complete set of matching tableware to set a festive table. You can buy salad or dessert plates with a holiday pattern, and use a white or complementary color dinner plate as a charger under the holiday plate. Accessorize with candles and glassware that you have on hand. Place greenery sprigs or berries along the center of the table, or fill a vase with fragrant pine and cedar for a centerpiece. Knot lengths of ribbon around napkins to act as napkin holders and to reinforce the color scheme.

SIMPLY GRAND

Using lots of your favorite things can produce a spectacular result. Here, a red table runner and place mats, white napkins and dinner plates, and green goblets and salad plates set the holiday mood. Silver containers and candlesticks shimmer as they reflect the Christmas tree lights. Rich red roses, berries, and lilies lend extravagance to the tabletop. Greenery sprigs tucked among the flowers define the arrangements as holiday decorations. Red candles and the wreath design on the napkins are good finishing touches. Remember to line silver containers with plastic bags or protective liners before filling them with water-soaked floral foam and flowers.

Classic Folds

Elevate an essential part of the table setting to prominence when you add a dash of panache to your napkin folds.

French Fold

1. Fold the napkin in half diagonally with the fold at the bottom.

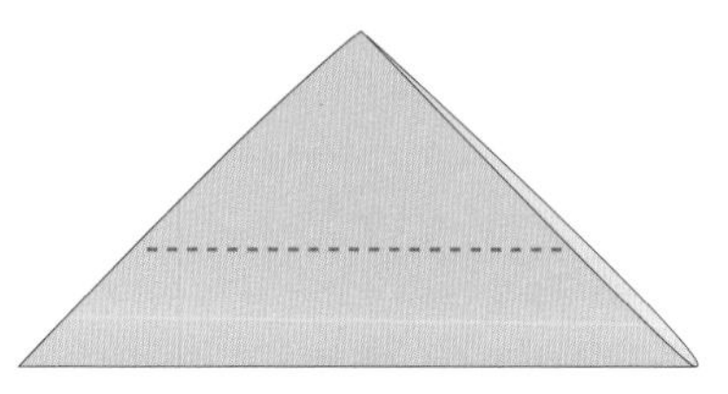

2. Fold up the bottom folded edge two-thirds toward the top point.

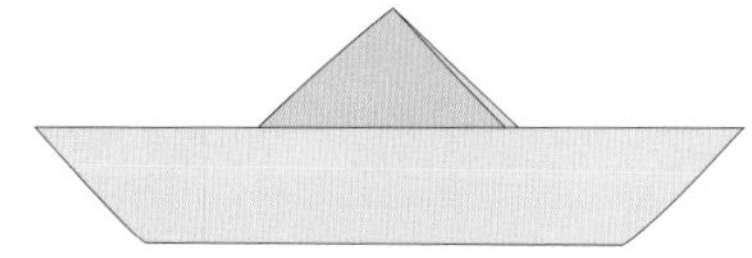

3. Beginning at one side of the bottom edge and working toward the other, pleat the napkin. Tuck the pleated end into a coffee cup.

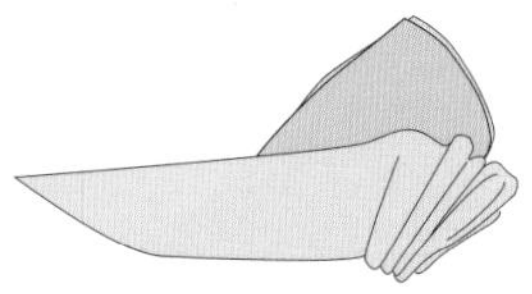

Neatly Tied

1. Fold the napkin in half diagonally with the fold at the bottom.

2. Holding the bottom folded edge at the center, fold the right and left points up toward the center point.

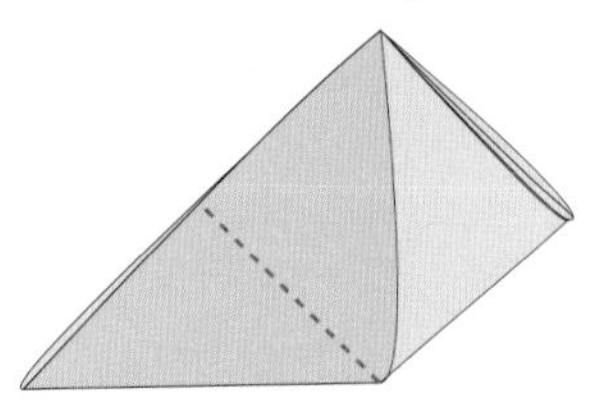

3. Fold the bottom point up to about one inch below the top point. Fold under the right and left sides. Tie a ribbon around the folded napkin, if desired.

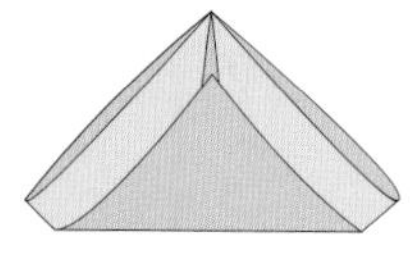

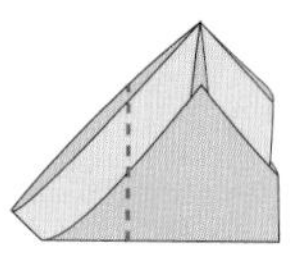

Poinsettia Points

1. Fold the corners of the napkin toward the center. Then, fold the new corners toward the center.

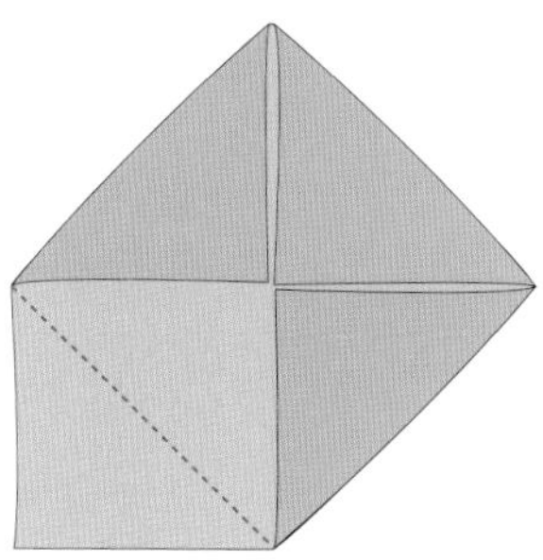

2. Turn the napkin over, keeping the center points together. Fold the corners toward the center.

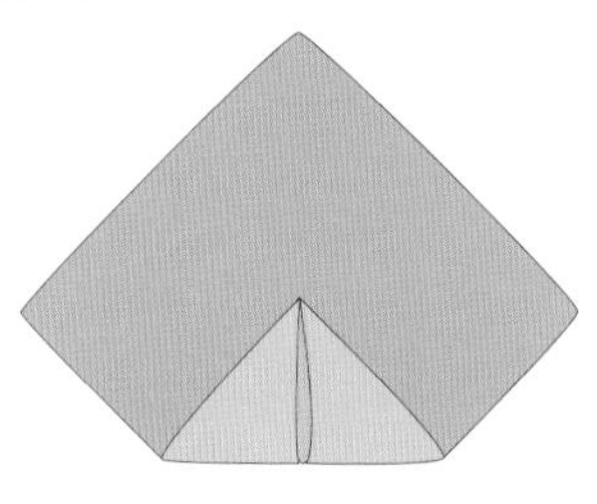

3. Holding the center securely, pull the corners out and up from the underside to make the points. Place an ornament or small gift box in the center of the napkin.

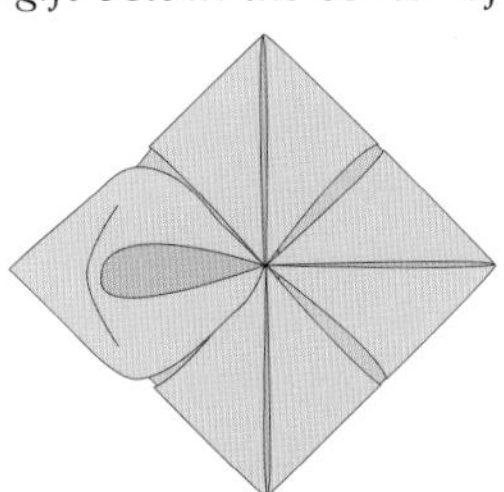

Pocket Fold

1. Fold the napkin in quarters. Position the napkin so that the free points are at the upper left corner.

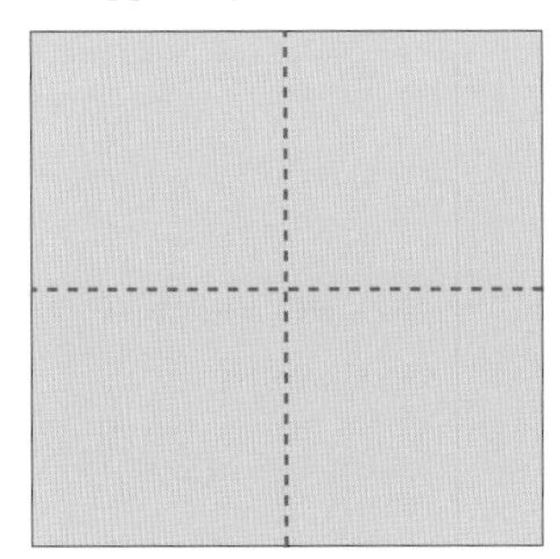

2. Fold the upper left corner of the top layer down toward the lower right corner.

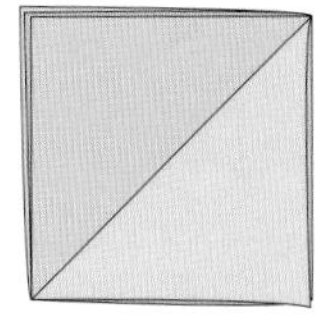

3. Fold under the top right and bottom left corners. Place silverware in the pocket.

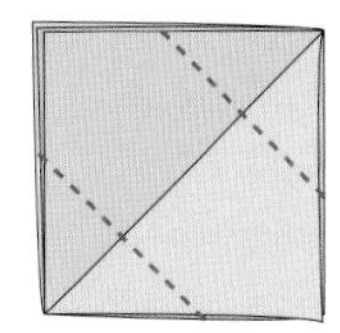

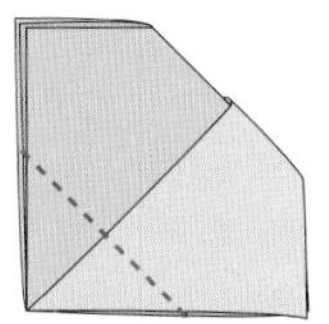

Fruit Centerpieces

An arrangement to grace the center of the table is a tribute to the specialness of the season. This year consider using fruit—a readily available and inexpensive alternative to flowers.

◀ Christmas Cheer

Red, green, and white are the colors of the season, and this stacked centerpiece shows them in a most refreshing way. For this design, fill a large bowl with floral foam. Use floral picks to secure apples into the foam around the edges of the bowl. Set a small bowl in the center of the large bowl and on top of the floral foam. Stack apples in the small bowl, and fill in the spaces with greenery and berry sprigs.

▲ Abundantly Appealing

Fruits in a variety of glorious colors and shapes add richness to this filled-to-overflowing display. Pears, apples, oranges, grapes, figs, limes, star fruits, and persimmons are used here, but this idea works well with almost any combination. The container is filled with floral foam, and larger pieces of fruit are anchored into the foam using floral picks. Smaller fruits fill in the spaces. Bits of moss provide texture.

▲ Simply Done

A single row of pears in a flat, rectangular dish form an amazingly stylish table decoration. A touch of greenery softens the arrangement; otherwise, silky brown cording tied around the stems is the only adornment needed.

Old World Charm

The holes in an antique sugar mold offer ideal receptacles for candles, fruits, and greenery. In lieu of a sugar mold, you can duplicate this arrangement using a rectangle of floral foam. Soak the floral foam in water, wrap it with chicken wire, and insert greenery and berries to cover the sides of the foam. Decorate the top with candles and an assortment of fruits and clippings. Use floral picks to secure the fruits into the foam. (To protect your tabletop, place the arrangement on a large platter or on plastic.) ▶

Sugar Mold Savvy

Sugar molds like the one pictured here can be found at antiques shops, but you may be surprised to learn that many home accessories stores carry reproductions, as well. *See page 170 for sources.*

Greenery from the Grocery

Now that many large food stores have floral departments, you can shop for centerpieces while you shop for menu items. Here, we show ideas for arranging supermarket blooms in astonishing ways.

◀ Winter White

Combine paperwhites, poinsettias, maidenhair fern, and azaleas for an impressive green and white grouping. Simply place the plants in their individual pots into a more spacious and decorative container, such as this large silver bucket. First, line the container with a plastic bag. Then position the larger elements—paperwhites, poinsettias, and azaleas—and fill in the open spaces with maidenhair fern. For a denser look, remove the plants from their pots and plant them in the decorative container.

▲ Chandelier Centerpiece

To decorate a chandelier like this, you need a light fixture that has a flat base where potted plants can sit without sliding or falling through. Small pots of poinsettias and paperwhites, accented with variegated holly and greenery, are used here. If your chandelier isn't suited for this style arrangement, try the same grouping on a tabletop for an equally striking centerpiece. Here, a single ivy topiary becomes an attractive centerpiece when placed on a table runner and surrounded with angels and candles.

Topiary Treat

For Christmas decoration and holiday gifts, consider the versatile live ivy topiary. Most grocery store floral departments carry these, but check the garden departments at home improvement centers and discount stores, as well.

Wound around a tree-shaped wire form, ivy makes a good backdrop or greenery filler in lots of seasonal arrangements. Place the topiary in its plastic pot into a decorative container for a delightfully quick gift. With the addition of wired ribbon and ornaments, it resembles a miniature Christmas tree. Once the holidays have passed, remove the embellishments, and the ivy carries on as a year-round houseplant.

Hat Trick

The bright red flowers and rich green leaves of kalanchoe make it an appropriate selection for the Christmas season. Dress up the plastic pot by using a straw hat as a creative planter. An ideal gift for a garden enthusiast, the plant will be appreciated and the hat "container" will be welcomed sun protection for the gardener in the spring.

Set the plant in a plastic or cellophane bag to protect the inside of the hat, and then place the bag in the hat. Tie ribbon around the edge of the hat and around the plant.

Poised Poinsettias

Showcase poinsettia's vibrant color by clustering several together for impact. Partnered with red candles, these festive flowers shout Christmas. If the plant's foil-wrapped plastic pot doesn't suit your decor, remove the plant and set it in a moss-lined glass container. Be sure to place poinsettias in bright, but not direct, sunlight for at least six hours a day and keep the soil moist with lukewarm water. When selecting your plant, look for one with tightly clustered buds and no evidence of pollen on the leaves.

WRAPPED ARRANGEMENT

A gift package of roses and appleberry bush makes a sprightly holiday centerpiece or a present for a favorite friend. The red and green florals and the bright plaid ribbon are a delightfully festive combination.

To begin, place a water-soaked block of floral foam in a plastic bag and set it in the tin. Cut the stems of roses short and insert them into the foam. Fill in open spaces with appleberry bush or backyard greenery clippings. Wrap ribbon around the sides of the tin, securing it to the foam with wired floral picks. Fold a long piece of ribbon into loops, pinch it together in the center and secure it with a wired floral pick. Insert the pick into the floral foam at the center and fluff the loops.

CASUAL HOLIDAY MEALS

Count on serving company or your family these stress-free holiday menus.

CHRISTMAS BREAKFAST

This festive morning meal includes everyone's favorites—eggs, sausage, biscuits, and fruit—in a delicious combination. The best feature is that much of the preparation can be done a day ahead.

MENU FOR 6 TO 8

Cream Cheese Scrambled Eggs

Sausage and Wild Rice Casserole

Ruby Pears • Cheese Biscuits

Banana Streusel Coffee Cake

Hot Percolator Punch

Ann Considine of Savannah, Georgia, and her family don't consider it Christmas until they've had "the breakfast." The Considines have been starting their Christmas celebration with this morning menu since 1981 when it first ran in *Southern Living® Annual Recipes*. "Our children are married now, but they come drifting back for the Christmas breakfast. The sausage casserole is our favorite," says Ann. Our Food staff recently retested and updated these recipes with today's tastes in mind to make them as dependable for your family as they have been for Ann's.

Casual Game Plan

Here's a bountiful menu to start the Christmas day festivities. Pick only recipes that appeal to you, or take advantage of the make-ahead components and prepare them all. Get the family involved in making biscuits and stirring the eggs. The sausage casserole and Ruby Pears can be started the night before. Then they can bake side by side before the biscuits. While baking biscuits, let the punch perk. And if anyone's still hungry after the meal's underway, a glazed coffee cake (that can be made a day ahead) awaits the sweet tooth.

Cream Cheese Scrambled Eggs

Cream cheese and some gentle stirring produce creamy results for this skilletful of eggs.

12 large eggs
1 cup half-and-half or milk
2 (3-ounce) packages cream cheese, cubed
¾ teaspoon salt
¼ teaspoon pepper
¼ cup butter or margarine
Chopped fresh chives

Process first 5 ingredients in a blender until frothy, stopping to scrape down sides.

Melt butter in a large heavy skillet over medium heat; reduce heat to medium-low. Add egg mixture, and cook, without stirring, until mixture begins to set on bottom. Draw a spatula across bottom of skillet to form large curds. Continue cooking until eggs are thickened but still moist; do not stir constantly. Sprinkle with chives. Yield: 6 to 8 servings.

Stirring eggs only a few times during cooking produces large, creamy curds.

Sausage and Wild Rice Casserole

This meaty casserole topped with toasted nuts makes a hearty contribution to breakfast.

1 (6-ounce) package long-grain and wild rice mix (we tested with Uncle Ben's)
1 pound hot ground pork sausage
1 pound ground beef
1 large onion, chopped
1 (8-ounce) package sliced fresh mushrooms
1 (8-ounce) can sliced water chestnuts, drained
⅓ cup chopped fresh parsley
3 tablespoons soy sauce
1 (2.25-ounce) package sliced natural almonds (½ cup)

Cook rice mix according to package directions.

Cook sausage and ground beef in a large skillet, stirring until it crumbles and is no longer pink. Drain and pat dry with paper towels. Cook onion and mushrooms in same skillet over medium heat 7 minutes or until tender, stirring occasionally.

Combine rice, sausage and beef, onion and mushrooms, water chestnuts, parsley, and soy sauce; stir well. Spoon mixture into an ungreased 13" x 9" baking dish. Cover and chill casserole overnight.

Remove from refrigerator, and let stand at room temperature 30 minutes. Sprinkle with almonds. Bake, uncovered, at 350° for 40 minutes or until thoroughly heated. Yield: 8 to 10 servings.

Note: *You don't have to refrigerate the casserole overnight. Just spoon it into the baking dish and bake, uncovered, at 350° for 20 minutes or until heated.*

Ruby Pears

Serve these easy pear halves warm or chilled. The sweet jelly glaze and dollop of thick cream topping are what make them so good.

2 (29-ounce) cans pear halves, drained
2 cups ginger ale
¼ cup fresh orange juice (about 1 orange)
2 tablespoons fresh lemon juice (about ½ lemon)
2 tablespoons butter or margarine, melted
½ teaspoon ground cinnamon, divided
1 (12-ounce) jar red currant jelly
Mock Devonshire Cream
Garnish: ground cinnamon

Cream Cheese Scrambled Eggs, Ruby Pears, Cheese Biscuits, Sausage and Wild Rice Casserole

Arrange pear halves, cut side up, in an ungreased 13" x 9" baking dish. Stir together ginger ale and next 3 ingredients. Pour ginger ale mixture over pears; sprinkle with ¼ teaspoon cinnamon. Cover and chill at least 3 hours or overnight.

Remove pears from refrigerator, and let stand at room temperature 30 minutes. Uncover and bake at 350° for 40 minutes.

Melt jelly in a small saucepan over low heat; stir in remaining ¼ teaspoon cinnamon and 3 tablespoons pan juices.

Remove pears from baking dish using a slotted spoon. Place pears in a serving dish; pour jelly mixture over pears. Serve with Mock Devonshire Cream. Garnish, if desired. Yield: 6 to 8 servings.

Mock Devonshire Cream

1 cup whipping cream
½ cup sour cream
2 tablespoons powdered sugar
1 teaspoon vanilla extract

Beat whipping cream at high speed with an electric mixer until soft peaks form; fold in sour cream, sugar, and vanilla. Yield: 2¾ cups.

Note: *Otherwise known as clotted cream, Devonshire cream is a specialty of Devonshire, England. It's made by heating rich, unpasteurized milk and, after cooling, removing the thickened cream that forms a top layer. In our version, sour cream mocks the thick texture of the real cream.*

Banana Streusel Coffee Cake
Hot Percolator Punch

Cheese Biscuits

A little mustard boosts the cheese flavor in these quick biscuits. Quick tip: Grate the cheese the night before.

2 cups self-rising flour
1 teaspoon dry mustard
6 tablespoons shortening
1 cup (4 ounces) shredded sharp Cheddar cheese
¾ cup buttermilk

Stir together flour and mustard; cut in shortening with a pastry blender until mixture is crumbly. Stir in cheese. Add buttermilk, stirring until dry ingredients are moistened. Turn dough out onto a lightly floured surface, and knead 3 or 4 times.

Roll dough to ¾" thickness; cut with a 2" biscuit cutter. Place biscuits on a lightly greased baking sheet.

Bake at 450° for 10 to 12 minutes or until lightly browned. Yield: 1 dozen.

Banana Streusel Coffee Cake

The yummy streusel's on the inside of this moist banana Bundt cake.

1 cup butter or margarine, softened
1½ cups sugar
2 large eggs
3 mashed ripe bananas (about 1⅓ cups)
1 teaspoon vanilla extract
2¼ cups all-purpose flour
1½ teaspoons baking powder
½ teaspoon baking soda
⅛ teaspoon salt
1 (8-ounce) container sour cream
¾ cup chopped pecans
2 tablespoons sugar
1 teaspoon ground cinnamon
1½ cups sifted powdered sugar
1 to 1½ tablespoons water

Beat butter at medium speed with an electric mixer until creamy; gradually add 1½ cups sugar, beating well. Add eggs, 1 at a time, beating until blended after each addition. Stir in banana and vanilla.

Combine flour and next 3 ingredients; add to butter mixture alternately with sour cream, beginning and ending with flour mixture. Beat at low speed until blended after each addition.

Rings of Old

It's a Southern thing to showcase our silver treasures. Use your family heirloom napkin rings for special occasions. These antique rings are numbered.

Combine pecans, 2 tablespoons sugar, and cinnamon. Pour half of batter into a greased and floured 12-cup Bundt pan; sprinkle with pecan mixture. Pour remaining batter over pecan layer. Bake at 350° for 50 minutes or until a long wooden pick inserted in center comes out clean. Cool in pan on a wire rack 10 minutes; remove from pan, and cool on wire rack.

Combine powdered sugar and water, stirring until smooth. Spoon glaze over cooled cake. Yield: 1 (10") cake.

Hot Percolator Punch

Here's a classic Southern Living *punch that sends an inviting cinnamon aroma throughout your house as it perks.*

3 cups unsweetened pineapple juice
3 cups cranberry-apple juice drink
1 cup water
⅓ cup firmly packed light brown sugar
2 lemon slices
2 (4") cinnamon sticks, broken
1½ teaspoons whole cloves
Cinnamon sticks (optional)

Pour juices and water into a 12-cup percolator. Place brown sugar and next 3 ingredients in percolator basket. Perk through complete cycle of electric percolator. Serve with cinnamon sticks, if desired. Yield: 7 cups.

Note: *This is an easy recipe to double if you have a larger percolator and a bigger crowd to serve.*

COUNTRY CHRISTMAS

Bring the mouthwatering goodness of country cooking back home. This Old South menu is sure to remind family and friends of the pleasure found in gathering for a holiday celebration filled with old-fashioned flavor.

MENU FOR 8

Brown Sugar Honey-Crusted Ham

Country Corn Relish

Homestyle Green Beans • Candied Sweet Potatoes and Apples

Biscuits or Rolls

Orange Pound Cake with Fresh Orange Syrup

Brown Sugar Honey-Crusted Ham, Country Corn Relish, Homestyle Green Beans, Candied Sweet Potatoes and Apples

Brown Sugar Honey-Crusted Ham

The sugar-crusted edge of baked ham is the best bite. This ham gets an extra sweet hit from honey.

1 (8-pound) smoked ham half (shank end)
⅔ cup honey
1 cup firmly packed light brown sugar
2 teaspoons ground nutmeg
1 teaspoon ground cloves
1 teaspoon ground cinnamon
Garnishes: lady apples and kumquats

Remove skin and excess fat from ham. Place ham, fat side up, on a rack in a shallow roasting pan lined with heavy-duty aluminum foil.

Bake, uncovered, at 325° for 1 hour and 15 minutes. Remove from oven.

Brush honey all over ham. Combine brown sugar and next 3 ingredients; pat sugar mixture over honey, coating ham thoroughly. Bake, uncovered, for 1 more hour or until a meat thermometer inserted into thickest part of ham registers 140°. Remove to a serving platter. Garnish, if desired. Yield: 12 to 14 servings.

Country Corn Relish

This refrigerator relish makes enough for you to enjoy and to give away a few jars as gifts. The relish is almost as good without tomatoes, if you can't find good produce in the winter.

2 (15¼-ounce) cans whole kernel corn, drained
4 green onions, thinly sliced
4 plum tomatoes, diced
1 medium-size green bell pepper, diced
⅓ cup vegetable oil
⅓ cup apple cider vinegar
1 tablespoon sugar
½ teaspoon dried basil
½ teaspoon dried parsley flakes
¼ teaspoon dried crushed red pepper

Stir together first 4 ingredients in a large bowl.

Whisk together oil and remaining 5 ingredients. Pour oil mixture over corn mixture, and stir gently to combine. Cover and chill least 3 hours. Yield: 6 cups.

Colorful Country Corn Relish makes a great gift at Christmas or anytime.

Candied Sweet Potatoes and Apples

Homestyle Green Beans

You can't beat old-fashioned green beans for a simple side dish that suits the whole family.

2 pounds fresh green beans, trimmed and cut into 1½" pieces
2 cups water
1 teaspoon salt
⅓ cup butter or margarine
1½ tablespoons sugar
1 teaspoon dried basil
½ teaspoon garlic powder
¼ teaspoon salt
¼ teaspoon pepper
2 cups halved cherry or grape tomatoes

Place beans in a Dutch oven; add water and salt. Bring to a boil; cover, reduce heat, and simmer 15 minutes or until tender. Drain; keep warm.

Melt butter in a saucepan over medium heat; stir in sugar and next 4 ingredients. Add tomato, and cook, stirring gently until thoroughly heated. Pour tomato mixture over beans, and toss gently. Serve hot. Yield: 8 servings.

Candied Sweet Potatoes and Apples

Prepare these candied vegetables a day ahead and chill them; then when the ham's finished baking, reheat the vegetables just before serving.

2 pounds sweet potatoes, peeled
1 cup firmly packed light brown sugar
1 cup butter or margarine
½ cup apple cider
¼ teaspoon salt
1 teaspoon vanilla extract
3 large Braeburn or other cooking apples, cored and cut into ½" rings

Cut sweet potatoes in half crosswise. Cook in boiling water to cover 10 minutes. Drain and cool. Cut crosswise into ½" slices.

Combine brown sugar and next 3 ingredients in a medium saucepan. Bring to a boil; boil 10 minutes. Remove from heat; stir in vanilla.

Layer sweet potato and apple slices in a greased 13" x 9" baking dish. Pour glaze over slices. Bake, uncovered, at 400° for 1 hour or until potatoes are candied and glaze is thickened, basting with glaze after 30 minutes. Yield: 8 servings.

Orange Pound Cake with Fresh Orange Syrup

Pound cake is the Southern dessert for all occasions. This orange-scented version makes a nice finish for the holiday meal.

1 cup butter, softened
2 cups sugar
4 large eggs
3 cups all-purpose flour
½ teaspoon baking soda
⅛ teaspoon salt
1 cup buttermilk
2 teaspoons orange extract
1 teaspoon vanilla extract
Powdered Sugar
Fresh Orange Syrup

Beat butter at medium speed with an electric mixer about 2 minutes or until creamy. Gradually add sugar, beating 5 to 7 minutes. Add eggs, 1 at a time, beating just until yellow disappears.

Combine flour, baking soda, and salt; add to butter mixture alternately with buttermilk, beginning and ending with flour mixture. Beat at low speed just until blended after each addition. Stir in flavorings. Pour batter into a greased and floured 10" tube pan.

Bake at 350° for 55 minutes or until a long wooden pick inserted in center comes out clean. Cool in pan on a wire rack 10 to 15 minutes; remove from pan, and cool on wire rack. Sprinkle with powdered sugar. Serve with Fresh Orange Syrup. Yield: 1 (10") cake.

Fresh Orange Syrup

1⅓ cups fresh orange juice (about 6 oranges)
1 cup sugar
1 tablespoon butter
1⅓ cups fresh orange sections (about 3 oranges)

Combine orange juice and sugar in a large nonaluminum skillet. Bring to a boil over medium heat, stirring constantly until sugar dissolves. Cook 17 minutes or until mixture is reduced to 1 cup. Remove from heat; add butter, stirring until butter melts. Gently stir in orange sections. Serve warm, or cover and chill. Stir gently just before serving. Store in an airtight container in refrigerator. Yield: 2 cups.

Carolers' Warm-Up

While caroling warms hearts, this robust menu satisfies appetites. Get started on the right note with mugs of Hot Spiced Wine for adults and hot cocoa for the children. Then serve filling chili and savory scones (make a double batch if your crowd is large), and be sure everyone grabs a crackle cookie as they head out the door.

Menu for 6

Hot Spiced Wine • Hot cocoa

Thick Three-Bean Chili

Cheddar Scones

Spicy Chocolate Crackles

Hot Spiced Wine

A quick version of mulled wine, this party drink highlights a wonderful blend of spice and citrus.

2 (3") cinnamon sticks
2 teaspoons whole cloves
1 teaspoon whole allspice
6 cups fruity red wine (such as Beaujolais or Pinot Noir)
6 cups apple cider
¾ cup sugar
1 orange, thinly sliced
1 lemon, thinly sliced
1 lime, thinly sliced

Place first 3 ingredients on an 8" square of cheesecloth; tie with string. Place spice bag in a Dutch oven. Add red wine and remaining 5 ingredients; bring to a simmer over low heat (do not boil). Keep at a simmer while serving. Ladle into mugs. Yield: 13 cups.

Note: *For a nonalcoholic version, omit wine and substitute more apple cider.*

Thick Three-Bean Chili

We liked the three beans used here, but you could use all kidney beans if you prefer.

1 pound ground round
1 medium onion, chopped
2 jalapeño peppers, seeded and chopped
2 tablespoons chili powder
2 teaspoons brown sugar
½ teaspoon ground red pepper
¼ teaspoon ground cumin
2 (15-ounce) cans tomato sauce
1 (6-ounce) can tomato paste
1¾ cups water
1¼ cups beer or beef broth
1 teaspoon apple cider vinegar
1 (16-ounce) can light red kidney beans, drained
1 (15.5-ounce) can butter beans, drained
1 (15-ounce) can chickpeas, drained
½ teaspoon salt

Cook ground round and onion in a Dutch oven over medium-high heat, stirring until meat crumbles and onion is tender; drain. Return to pan.

Add jalapeño pepper and next 4 ingredients; cook 2 minutes. Add tomato sauce and next 4 ingredients; stir well. Stir in beans. Bring to a boil; reduce heat, and simmer, uncovered, over medium-low heat 45 minutes, stirring occasionally. Stir in salt before serving. Yield: about 11 cups.

Thick Three-Bean Chili
Cheddar Scone

SPICY CHOCOLATE CRACKLES

Ground ginger and pepper (yes, pepper) spice up this sugar-coated cookie kids will like.

1 (18.25-ounce) package devil's food cake mix
⅓ cup vegetable oil
2 large eggs, lightly beaten
1 tablespoon ground ginger
½ teaspoon ground pepper
1 tablespoon water
½ cup semisweet chocolate mini-morsels
¼ cup sugar

Combine first 6 ingredients in a large bowl, stirring until smooth. Stir in mini-morsels.

Shape dough into 1" balls; roll in sugar to coat. Place balls 2" apart on lightly greased baking sheets.

Bake at 375° for 9 minutes. Cool 2 to 3 minutes on baking sheets. Remove to wire racks to cool completely. Yield: 4 dozen.

CHEDDAR SCONES

These light-textured little wedges of cheese bread are ideal for dunking into a steaming bowl of chili. They're also good for breakfast.

1¾ cups all-purpose flour
1 tablespoon sugar
2 teaspoons baking powder
¾ teaspoon salt
¼ cup cold butter, cut into pieces
1 cup (4 ounces) finely shredded sharp Cheddar cheese
1 large egg, lightly beaten
⅔ cup half-and-half
1 tablespoon butter, melted

Combine first 4 ingredients in a large bowl; cut in cold butter with a pastry blender until mixture is crumbly. Stir in cheese.

Stir together egg and half-and-half. Gradually add to flour mixture, stirring with a fork just until dry ingredients are moistened. Turn dough out onto a lightly floured surface, and knead 3 or 4 times. Gently roll into a ball.

Pat dough into a 7" circle on an ungreased baking sheet. Cut into 6 wedges, using a sharp knife. (Do not separate wedges.)

Bake at 400° for 16 to 18 minutes or until golden. Remove from oven; brush with 1 tablespoon melted butter. Serve warm. Yield: 6 scones.

Manicotti Night

Manicotti is a filling main dish, one you can make ahead and count on for company. This rich meatless version partners well with a beautiful, fresh green salad. And the dessert's easy—make the cookies ahead and pick up some sorbet at the market.

Menu for 6

Field Greens with Tangerine Dressing and Pesto Wafers

Shiitake Mushroom and Spinach Manicotti • Pistachio Shortbread Crisps

Field Greens with Tangerine Dressing

Field Greens with Tangerine Dressing and Pesto Wafers

A lively citrus dressing and some crisp cheese wafers adorn this bowl of greens.

1/3 cup loosely packed fresh basil leaves
2 tablespoons pine nuts
1 garlic clove, halved
3 ounces freshly grated Parmigiano-Reggiano cheese
6 cups loosely packed gourmet mixed salad greens
Tangerine Dressing
3 tangerines, sectioned
1/2 small purple onion, halved and thinly sliced

Combine first 3 ingredients in a food processor or blender; process until smooth, stopping to scrape down sides. Stir together basil mixture and grated cheese in a small bowl.

Place a 1 1/2" round cutter on a lightly greased baking sheet. Sprinkle 1 tablespoon cheese mixture into cutter. Press cheese into cutter; remove cutter. Repeat procedure with remaining cheese mixture, spacing wafers 2" apart. Bake at 350° for 10 to 12 minutes or until edges are browned. Cool 30 seconds on baking sheet. Remove to wire racks to cool completely.

Toss salad greens with Tangerine Dressing. Add tangerine sections and onion slices. Serve with cheese wafers. Yield: 6 servings.

Tangerine Dressing

1/3 cup fresh tangerine juice (about 2 large tangerines)
2 tablespoons extra-virgin olive oil
1 tablespoon white wine vinegar
1 tablespoon honey
2 teaspoons minced shallot
1/4 teaspoon salt

Whisk together all ingredients. Yield: 1/2 cup.

Going, Going, Gone

These thin, crisp pesto wafers may just be the highlight of the meal. (They're part of the salad recipe.) You won't be able to stop at just one.

SHIITAKE MUSHROOM AND SPINACH MANICOTTI

This creamy, crusty-topped casserole is a great make-ahead option for the holiday rush.

12 manicotti or cannelloni shells
¼ cup butter or margarine, divided
4½ cups sliced fresh shiitake or other mushrooms (8 ounces)
2 garlic cloves, minced
1 (10-ounce) package fresh spinach, coarse stems removed
1 cup ricotta cheese
3 ounces freshly grated Parmesan cheese
1 large egg, beaten
½ teaspoon salt
½ teaspoon freshly ground pepper
⅓ cup butter or margarine
2 tablespoons all-purpose flour
2 cups half-and-half
½ teaspoon salt
1 cup (4 ounces) shredded Gouda cheese
2 7-grain sandwich bread slices (we tested with Branola)
1½ cups (6 ounces) shredded Mexican four-cheese blend
3 tablespoons butter or margarine, melted

Cook shells according to package directions; drain.

Meanwhile, melt 3 tablespoons butter in a large skillet; add mushrooms and garlic, and sauté until mushroom liquid is absorbed. Transfer mushroom mixture to a large bowl.

Melt remaining 1 tablespoon butter in skillet. Add spinach; cover and cook over medium-low heat 5 minutes or until spinach wilts. Add spinach to mushroom mixture. Stir in ricotta cheese and next 4 ingredients. Spoon spinach mixture evenly into shells. Place stuffed shells in a greased 13" x 9" baking dish.

Melt ⅓ cup butter in a heavy saucepan over low heat; whisk in flour until smooth. Cook 1 minute, whisking constantly. Gradually whisk in half-and half; cook over medium heat, whisking constantly, until mixture is thickened and bubbly. Stir in ½ teaspoon salt. Add Gouda cheese, stirring until cheese melts. Pour over stuffed shells.

Process bread in a blender or food processor until it resembles coarse crumbs. Spread crumbs in a small pan; bake at 350° for 3 to 4 minutes or until toasted. Combine toasted crumbs, cheese blend, and 3 tablespoons melted butter in a bowl; toss well, and sprinkle over shells.

Bake, uncovered, at 350° for 45 minutes or until bubbly. Yield: 6 servings.

Note: *If desired, cover and chill manicotti at least 8 hours before baking. Remove from refrigerator, and let stand at room temperature 30 minutes. Bake as directed.*

PISTACHIO SHORTBREAD CRISPS

Serve these thick, crisp, nutty cookies with lemon sorbet or vanilla ice cream.

1 cup butter, softened
½ cup sugar
2 teaspoons vanilla extract
2 cups all-purpose flour
1 cup pistachio nuts
Sugar

Beat butter at medium speed with an electric mixer until creamy; gradually add ½ cup sugar, beating well. Add vanilla, beating until blended. Gradually add flour, beating just until combined.

Process pistachios in a food processor until coarsely ground. Place ground nuts on a plate.

Shape dough into 1" balls. Working over plate of nuts with 1 ball at a time, sprinkle about 1 tablespoon nuts over ball, pressing nuts gently into ball. Repeat procedure with remaining balls and nuts. Place balls on ungreased baking sheets; flatten to ⅜" thickness. Sprinkle with sugar.

Bake at 350° for 10 minutes or until lightly browned. Immediately remove to wire racks to cool completely. Yield: about 2½ dozen.

Cocktail Hour

Set out an assortment of these Mediterranean-inspired hors d'oeuvres along with your favorite wines, cheeses, and fruit, and you've got a holiday happy hour ready and waiting. Both relishes and pita toasts can be made ahead.

Menu for 12 or more

Roasted Onions, Figs, and Smoked Sausage

Kalamata Olive Relish • Green Olive Relish

Toasted Pita Wedges

Walnut-Basil Pastries with Dried Tomatoes

Prosciutto Crab Cakes with Red Pepper Mayonnaise

Assorted fruit and cheeses

Red and white wines

Fruit and Cheese Tray

Embellish this party spread with red and green grapes, crisp apples and pears, a combination of hard and soft cheeses, some nuts, and breadsticks.

Roasted Onions, Figs, and Smoked Sausage

Roasted Onions, Figs, and Smoked Sausage

This serving bowl holds a roasted antipasto option. Set out forks for your guests.

1 (8-ounce) package dried figs, quartered
½ cup apricot nectar
¼ cup honey
2 tablespoons balsamic vinegar
1 teaspoon chopped fresh rosemary
1 pound kielbasa or other smoked sausage, cut into ½" slices
2 cups coarsely chopped onion
2 small sweet potatoes, peeled and cut into 1" pieces (about 2½ cups)

Combine first 3 ingredients in a small saucepan. Bring to a boil; cover and cook 1 minute. Remove from heat, and let stand 30 minutes. Stir in vinegar and rosemary; set aside.

Combine sausage, onion, and sweet potato in a large greased roasting pan. Bake, uncovered, at 450° for 30 minutes, stirring occasionally.

Stir fig mixture into sausage mixture; bake 10 more minutes. Serve warm or at room temperature. Yield: 12 appetizer servings.

Kalamata Olive Relish

This relish has a chunky texture thanks to whole nuts and olives chopped by hand.

2 tablespoons pine nuts
¼ cup dried tomatoes in oil, undrained
½ cup minced onion
1 tablespoon minced garlic
2 teaspoons dried basil
1 (8-ounce) jar kalamata olives, drained, pitted, and chopped

Bake nuts in a shallow pan at 350°, stirring occasionally, 5 minutes or until toasted. Drain dried tomatoes, reserving 2 tablespoons oil. Coarsely chop tomatoes.

Sauté onion in reserved oil in a large skillet over medium-high heat 5 minutes or until tender. Add garlic and sauté 1 minute. Add tomato and basil. Process tomato mixture in a blender or food processor 5 seconds or until almost pureed; place in a small bowl. Stir in olives and pine nuts. Cover and chill relish up to 1 week. Serve relish at room temperature. Yield: 2 cups.

Green Olive Relish

All the ingredients for this relish are blended in a food processor, producing a fine-textured finish.

2 garlic cloves
1 (7-ounce) jar pimiento-stuffed olives, drained
⅓ cup chopped fresh parsley
2 tablespoons olive oil
2 teaspoons lemon juice
1 teaspoon anchovy paste

Process garlic in a food processor until minced. Add olives and remaining ingredients; process until olives are finely chopped. Cover and chill relish up to 1 week. Serve relish at room temperature. Yield: 1¼ cups.

Toasted Pita Wedges

3 (6") pita bread rounds, split
Olive oil-flavored cooking spray

Cut each bread half into 8 wedges.

Place wedges in a single layer on an ungreased baking sheet; spray lightly with cooking spray. Bake at 350° for 6 to 8 minutes or until crisp. Yield: 4 dozen.

Kalamata Olive Relish
Green Olive Relish
Toasted Pita Wedges

WALNUT-BASIL PASTRIES WITH DRIED TOMATOES

Savory Mediterranean flavors fill these flaky pastry triangles.

16 frozen 14"-x 18" phyllo pastry sheets, thawed in refrigerator
¾ cup butter, melted
8 (1-ounce) slices provolone cheese, quartered
Walnut-Ricotta Spread
14 dried tomatoes in oil, drained and coarsely chopped
Garnish: fresh basil sprigs

Place 2 sheets of phyllo on a work surface (keeping remaining phyllo covered). Brush top sheet with melted butter. Cut buttered phyllo sheets lengthwise into 4 equal strips (about 3½" wide). Place 1 piece of provolone (folded, if necessary) onto 1 end of each strip. Spoon a scant tablespoon of Walnut-Ricotta Spread over cheese; top with a few pieces of dried tomato.

Working with 1 strip at a time, fold bottom corner of phyllo over filling, forming a triangle. Continue folding back and forth to end of strip. Lightly brush phyllo triangle with butter to seal. Repeat procedure with remaining phyllo (2 sheets at a time), butter, provolone, Walnut-Ricotta Spread, and dried tomatoes.

Place pastries on an ungreased baking sheet. Bake at 425° for 10 to 11 minutes or until evenly browned. Serve warm or at room temperature. Garnish, if desired. Yield: 32 pastries.

WALNUT-RICOTTA SPREAD

2 small garlic cloves
1 cup ricotta cheese
¾ cup grated Parmesan cheese
1 teaspoon sugar
½ cup chopped walnuts
12 fresh basil leaves, sliced
1 tablespoon olive oil
½ teaspoon salt
¼ teaspoon pepper

With food processor running, drop garlic cloves through food chute; process until minced. Add cheeses and sugar; process until smooth, stopping to scrape down sides. Add walnuts, basil, olive oil, salt, and pepper; process until blended. Yield: 1½ cups.

Walnut-Basil Pastries with Dried Tomatoes

Prosciutto Crab Cakes with Red Pepper Mayonnaise

Prosciutto (salt-cured Italian ham) is a nice surprise in these meaty cakes. Country ham makes a suitable substitute.

1 pound fresh lump crabmeat, drained
½ cup shaved prosciutto, finely chopped
½ cup French breadcrumbs (homemade)
1 large egg, lightly beaten
2 tablespoons grated onion
2 teaspoons white wine Worcestershire sauce
½ teaspoon salt
2 tablespoons butter or margarine, melted
2 tablespoons vegetable oil
Red Pepper Mayonnaise
Garnish: lemon slices

Combine crabmeat, prosciutto, and breadcrumbs in a bowl. Toss gently.

Stir together egg and next 3 ingredients in a small bowl. Gently fold egg mixture into crabmeat. Cover and chill at least ½ hour. Shape mixture into 12 patties, using a scant ¼ cupful for each. Place patties on a wax paper-lined baking sheet; cover and chill at least 1 hour.

Cook 6 patties in 1 tablespoon butter and 1 tablespoon oil in a large nonstick skillet over medium-high heat 5 to 6 minutes on each side or until browned. Remove from skillet; set aside, and keep warm. Repeat procedure with remaining patties, butter, and oil. Serve warm with Red Pepper Mayonnaise. Garnish, if desired. Yield: 12 crab cakes.

Red Pepper Mayonnaise

2 garlic cloves
⅓ cup drained and diced roasted sweet red peppers
½ teaspoon fresh lemon juice
⅛ teaspoon ground red pepper
1 cup mayonnaise, divided

With food processor running, drop garlic through food chute. Add diced pepper, lemon juice, ground pepper, and ¼ cup mayonnaise. Process 1 minute or until very smooth, stopping to scrape down sides. Transfer to a bowl; stir in remaining ¾ cup mayonnaise. Cover and chill at least 8 hours. Yield: 1⅓ cups.

WINTER HARVEST SUPPER

Savor the holiday season with a celebration featuring nature's bountiful food gifts. Begin the feast with ginger-kissed bowls of butternut soup. Then feast on a platter of mustard-crusted pork and roasted potatoes. Decorate each plate with glistening cranapple sauce. And for dessert, offer our dressed-up apple pie.

MENU FOR 6 TO 8

Butternut Squash Soup

Mustard-Crusted Pork Roast and Browned Potatoes

Cinnamon-Scented Cranapple Sauce

Green Bean Casserole with Fried Leeks

Dinner rolls

Cornmeal Streusel Apple Pie

Mustard-Crusted Pork Roast and Browned Potatoes

Butternut Squash Soup

This velvety starter soup is a blend of pureed squash and carrots, cream, and a hint of ginger.

1 (3-pound) butternut squash
¾ pound carrots, scraped and cut into chunks (8 carrots)
2½ cups chicken broth
¾ cup orange juice
½ teaspoon salt
½ teaspoon ground ginger
½ cup whipping cream
2 tablespoons finely chopped pecans, toasted
Ground nutmeg

Cut squash in half lengthwise; remove seeds. Place squash, cut sides down, in a shallow pan; add hot water to pan to depth of ¾". Cover with aluminum foil, and bake at 400° for 40 minutes or until tender; drain. Scoop out pulp; mash. Discard shell. Cook carrot in boiling water 25 minutes or until tender; drain and mash.

Combine squash, carrot, chicken broth, and next 3 ingredients in a bowl. Process half of mixture in a food processor or blender until smooth. Repeat procedure with remaining half of squash mixture.

Place pureed mixture in a large saucepan; bring to a simmer. Stir in cream; return to a simmer. Remove from heat. To serve, ladle into individual bowls. Sprinkle with pecans and nutmeg. Yield: 8 cups.

Mustard-Crusted Pork Roast and Browned Potatoes

A mustardy glaze locks moisture in this pork roast. Rosemary potatoes roast alongside the pork, making a rustic side dish.

1 (4-to 5-pound) boneless pork loin roast
¼ teaspoon salt
¼ teaspoon pepper
½ cup coarse-grained mustard
8 garlic cloves, minced
3 tablespoons olive oil
3 tablespoons balsamic vinegar
2 tablespoons chopped fresh rosemary
2 pounds new potatoes
2 tablespoons olive oil
1 tablespoon chopped fresh rosemary
½ teaspoon salt
½ teaspoon pepper
Garnish: fresh rosemary sprigs

Place pork in a greased roasting pan. Rub with ¼ teaspoon each salt and pepper. Combine mustard and next 4 ingredients in a small bowl; spread evenly over pork.

Peel a crosswise stripe around each potato with a vegetable peeler, if desired. Cut each potato in half lengthwise. Toss potatoes with 2 tablespoons oil, 1 tablespoon chopped rosemary, ½ teaspoon salt, and ½ teaspoon pepper. Add to roasting pan around pork. Insert meat thermometer into thickest part of roast.

Bake at 375° for 1 hour to 1¼ hours or until thermometer registers 160°. Let stand 10 minutes. Transfer roast to a serving platter. Surround pork with potatoes. Garnish, if desired. Yield: 8 servings.

Cinnamon-Scented Cranapple Sauce

Cinnamon-Scented Cranapple Sauce

This jewel-toned cranberry sauce gets embellished with tart apple, cinnamon pears, and citrus. It's a wonderful match for pork roast or turkey.

1 (16-ounce) can whole-berry cranberry sauce
1 (15-ounce) can cinnamon-flavored pear halves, drained and chopped
1 (11-ounce) can mandarin orange segments, drained
1 Granny Smith apple, peeled and chopped
1 cup sugar
½ cup dried fruit mix (we tested with Mariani Harvest Medley)

Combine all ingredients in a large saucepan; cook, uncovered, over medium-low heat 45 minutes or until thickened, stirring often. Remove sauce from heat; cover and chill.

Serve as an accompaniment to pork or turkey, or as a topping over vanilla ice cream, pound cake, or pancakes. Yield: 3½ cups.

Note: *If you can't find cinnamon-flavored pears, use regular canned pear halves and add ½ teaspoon ground cinnamon.*

Mustard-Crusted Pork Roast and Browned Potatoes,
Cinnamon-Scented Cranapple Sauce,
Green Bean Casserole with Fried Leeks

Green Bean Casserole with Fried Leeks

Remember the old green bean casserole made with convenience products: frozen or canned green beans, cream of mushroom soup, and French fried onions? Here it is again, only updated with some upscale ingredients.

2 tablespoons butter or margarine
2 (8-ounce) packages sliced fresh mushrooms
1 teaspoon dried thyme
2 shallots, finely chopped
½ cup Madeira
1 cup whipping cream
1¼ pounds fresh green beans, trimmed
Vegetable or peanut oil
2 large leeks, cleaned and thinly sliced crosswise
Salt

Melt butter in large heavy skillet over medium-high heat. Add mushrooms and thyme; sauté 5 minutes. Add shallots; sauté 3 minutes or until tender. Add Madeira, and cook over medium-high heat 3 minutes or until liquid evaporates. Add whipping cream, and cook 2 to 5 minutes or until slightly thickened. Remove from heat.

Meanwhile, cook beans in a small amount of boiling water 5 minutes or just until crisp-tender; drain. Add beans to mushroom mixture, and toss gently. Spoon into a greased 2-quart gratin dish or shallow baking dish. Cover and keep warm.

Pour oil to depth of 2" into a 3-quart saucepan; heat to 350°. Fry leeks in 3 batches, 40 seconds or until golden. Remove leeks with small metal strainer; drain on paper towels. Immediately sprinkle with salt. Sprinkle fried leeks over warm bean mixture. Bake, uncovered, at 400° for 5 minutes or until casserole is thoroughly heated. Yield: 6 servings.

CORNMEAL STREUSEL APPLE PIE

Dress up a storebought fruit pie with our Southern cornmeal streusel. Your guests will think the whole thing's from scratch, especially since you'll serve it from your own pieplate.

- ½ cup chopped walnuts
- ½ cup firmly packed light brown sugar
- 3 tablespoons all-purpose flour
- 3 tablespoons yellow cornmeal
- ¾ teaspoon ground cinnamon
- ¼ teaspoon ground nutmeg
- ½ cup (2 ounces) shredded sharp Cheddar cheese
- ⅓ cup unsalted butter, slightly softened
- 1 (3-pound, 1-ounce) frozen deep-dish apple pie (we tested with Mrs. Smith's)

Stir together first 6 ingredients in a medium bowl; stir in cheese. Gently work in butter with fingertips until mixture forms large crumbs. Cover and chill 30 minutes.

Meanwhile, remove frozen pie from aluminum pieplate and place in an ungreased 10" deep-dish pieplate. Cut slits in top crust according to package directions. Bake, uncovered, at 375° for 50 minutes. Remove from oven. Sprinkle cornmeal streusel over pie, mounding slightly in center. Bake, uncovered, 20 to 25 more minutes or until browned and bubbly. Cool in pieplate on a wire rack at least 30 minutes before serving. Yield: 1 (10") pie.

1. Remove frozen pie from aluminum pieplate and place in a glass or ceramic pieplate for baking. (This makes the pie look special and more homemade).

2. Sprinkle cornmeal streusel over partially baked pie, mounding in center. Finish baking.

Cornmeal Streusel Apple Pie

FRENCH NOËL

This elegant menu, starring roast goose and a dazzling chocolate cake, makes a grand presentation. The meal's origins are French, but many of the same foods are enjoyed in the American South—oysters, cabbage, green beans, and potatoes. If your clan's not fond of goose, just roast your traditional turkey, and serve these sides.

MENU FOR 8

Champagne

Fried Oyster and Pear Salad • French bread

Roast Goose with Currant Sauce

Sautéed Red Cabbage

French Green Beans with Basil and Orange

Scalloped Potatoes

Mocha-Orange Bûche de Noël

Cheers

The French like to celebrate the Christmas feast very early on Christmas morning, usually just after returning from midnight mass. Referred to as Reveillon, *this celebration means to begin a new watch or to awaken. The menu varies according to the region of France, but certain foods like oysters, a roast bird, and a chocolate Yule log are traditional. It's likely that the celebration begins with a champagne toast.*

Scalloped Potatoes, French Green Beans with Basil and Orange, Roast Goose with Currant Sauce, Sautéed Red Cabbage

Claude

Nicole

Bread Bags

In the French country style, place an individual sack of bread at each place setting. To make sacks, cut off and discard top half of lunch sacks; then roll cut edges down twice, creating cuffs. Write names on sacks, if desired. Line sacks with decorative paper napkins, and add bread.

FRIED OYSTER AND PEAR SALAD

This showy French salad (shown on previous page) has much to offer—fresh greens, juicy pears, crisp fried oysters, and a honey-balsamic vinaigrette. It's also good without oysters.

¾ cup olive oil
⅓ cup white balsamic vinegar
2 tablespoons honey
1 teaspoon herbes de Provence*
½ teaspoon salt
¼ teaspoon pepper
¾ cup yellow cornmeal
¼ cup all-purpose flour
¾ teaspoon salt
2 (12-ounce) containers fresh Select oysters, drained
Vegetable oil
8 cups loosely packed gourmet mixed salad greens
3 green onions, thinly sliced
3 ripe red Bartlett pears, unpeeled and thinly sliced

Whisk together first 6 ingredients; set aside.

Combine cornmeal, flour, and ¾ teaspoon salt. Dredge oysters in cornmeal mixture. Pour oil to depth of 2" into a Dutch oven; heat to 375°. Fry oysters, a few at a time, 2 minutes or until golden, turning once. Drain on paper towels. Set aside, and keep warm.

Arrange greens, green onions, pear slices, and oysters on individual plates. Drizzle dressing over salads. Serve immediately. Yield: 8 servings.

Note: *Fry the oysters ahead; then reheat them just before serving in a 450° oven for 3 to 5 minutes or until crisp.*

** Herbes de Provence is a dried herb blend consisting of herbs common to southern France. Find the blend in tiny earthenware crocks in specialty kitchen shops. For a simplified substitution, use ½ teaspoon each crushed lavender and rosemary leaves.*

The Story of Santons

The word santon means "little saint." These clay figures clad in Provençal costumes were often modeled after local townspeople and placed with great reverence at the Christmas crèche. Santons became widespread during the late 1700s and are considered collectors' items today. They're celebrated throughout the south of France at fall and winter fairs. Some collectors choose to display their Provençal dolls on mantels or as part of a centerpiece (as we did on the previous page).

Roast Goose with Currant Sauce

The procedure shown below for prepping and roasting this goose produces ultracrisp skin and moist meat.

1 (9- to 11-pound) dressed goose
1 tablespoon salt
1 tablespoon pepper
1 orange, quartered
1 medium onion, cut into wedges
1 carrot, cut into 4 pieces
1 bay leaf
Currant Sauce

Remove loose fat from goose cavity. Remove giblets and neck; reserve for other uses. Chop off wings just below the elbow, if desired. Rinse goose thoroughly with cold water; pat dry with paper towels. Using a trussing needle or sharp skewer, prick skin all over, especially around lower breast and thighs, holding the needle almost parallel to the goose to avoid piercing the meat (photo 1).

Add water to a tall stockpot, filling two-thirds full; bring to a rolling boil. Gently lower goose into boiling water, neck end down (photo 2); boil 1 to 2 minutes or until "goose bumps" appear. Remove goose, and repeat procedure, submerging goose tail end down. Drain; pat goose dry with paper towels. Place goose, breast side up, on a rack in a broiler pan. Refrigerate, uncovered, 24 to 48 hours (photo 3). (The longer you air-dry the goose, the crispier the skin will be after roasting).

Combine salt and pepper. Rub all over goose and inside cavity. Place orange and next 3 ingredients inside body cavity of goose. Place goose, breast side down, on a lightly greased rack in a roasting pan. Roast at 325° for 1½ hours. Remove goose from oven. Drain and discard grease from pan. Return goose, breast side up, to rack in pan; roast 1½ hours. Increase oven temperature to 400°, and roast 15 more minutes or until skin is very crisp and thermometer inserted into thigh registers 180°. Remove goose from oven. Let stand 20 minutes before carving. Serve with Currant Sauce. Yield: 8 servings.

Currant Sauce

½ cup red currant jelly
½ cup dry red wine (we tested with Burgundy)
¼ cup ketchup
¼ cup butter
2 tablespoons Worcestershire sauce
2 teaspoons cornstarch
¼ teaspoon dry mustard

Combine all ingredients in a small saucepan. Bring to a boil over medium heat, stirring constantly; cook 1 minute. Yield: 2 cups.

Getting Acquainted with Goose

Goose is prized for its crisp skin and flavorful all-dark meat. Most dressed geese in American markets weigh between 8 and 12 pounds. Most geese come to the market frozen, so allow 24 hours or more to thaw the bird in the refrigerator.

Follow these steps, and goose is easy to carve:

- Remove the leg on the side nearest you.
- Remove wing.
- Working on the side nearest you, cut down the whole length of the breast bone, removing the breast half in one piece.
- Lay breast meat flat on cutting board and slice on the diagonal, about ¼" thick.
- Repeat on other side of goose.

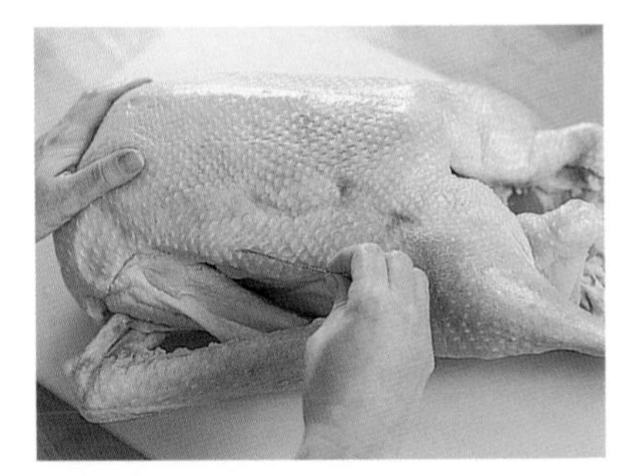

1. Prick skin, especially around the breast and thighs, holding needle almost parallel to the bird to avoid piercing meat.

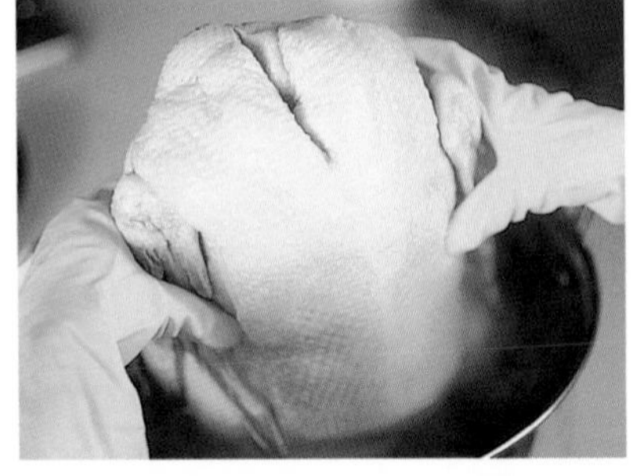

2. Carefully submerge goose into stockpot of boiling water. (Wear rubber gloves to protect your hands, if desired.)

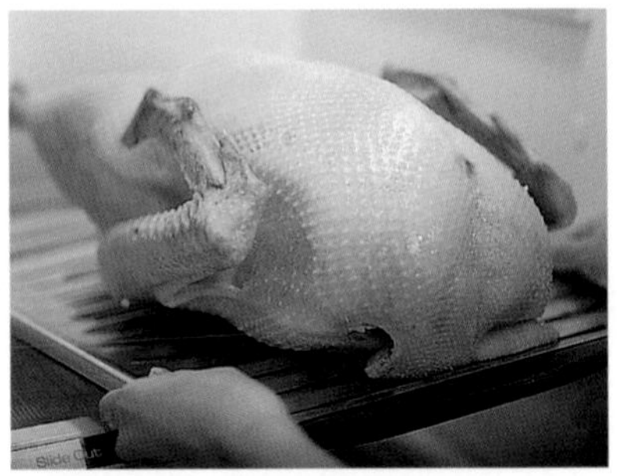

3. Place goose, uncovered, in refrigerator to dry out for 24 to 48 hours.

Cake Roll Clamor

We in the American South have a fondness for rolled cakes. They look pretty on a plate, they store easily, and you can garnish them in a number of ways. This French sponge cake made to resemble a log reminds us Southerners of a similar cake roll called roulage, *which is traditionally a chocolate cake filled and often frosted with whipped cream, and sometimes served partially frozen.*

Mocha-Orange Bûche de Noël

This traditional French Christmas cake isn't hard to make. The cake is a basic sponge cake, and once it's in the oven, the icing's a breeze. The fun comes when you fill, roll, and frost the cake, and it takes on the look of a log.

1 cup all-purpose flour
1 teaspoon baking powder
¼ teaspoon salt
4 large eggs, separated
¾ cup sugar, divided
⅓ cup water
1 tablespoon grated orange rind
1 teaspoon vanilla extract
1 teaspoon orange extract
3 tablespoons powdered sugar
4 teaspoons instant coffee granules
6 tablespoons milk
3¾ cups sifted powdered sugar
½ cup cocoa
6 tablespoons butter, softened
Garnishes: kumquats with leaves and fresh cranberries

Grease bottom and sides of a 15" x 10" jellyroll pan; line with wax paper; grease and flour wax paper. Set aside.

Combine flour, baking powder, and salt, stirring well. Set aside.

Beat egg whites at high speed with an electric mixer until foamy. Gradually add ¼ cup sugar, 1 tablespoon at a time, beating until stiff peaks form and sugar dissolves (2 to 4 minutes). Set aside.

Beat egg yolks in a large mixing bowl at high speed, gradually adding ½ cup sugar; beat 5 minutes or until thick and pale. Add water, orange rind, and flavorings; beat well. Add flour mixture, and beat just until blended. Fold in about one-third of egg white mixture. Gently fold in remaining egg white mixture. Spread batter evenly into prepared pan.

Bake at 375° for 10 minutes or until top springs back when lightly touched.

Sift 3 tablespoons powdered sugar in a 15" x 10" rectangle on a cloth towel; set aside. When cake is done, immediately loosen from sides of pan, and turn out onto sugared towel. Peel off wax paper. Starting at narrow end,

roll up cake and towel together; cool completely on a wire rack, seam side down.

While cake cools, stir coffee granules into milk until coffee granules dissolve. Combine 3¾ cups powdered sugar and cocoa in a large bowl, stirring well with a wire whisk. Add coffee mixture and butter to sugar mixture; beat at medium speed until smooth.

Unroll cake and remove towel. Spread cake with half of frosting; carefully reroll. Cut a 1" thick diagonal slice from 1 end of cake roll. Place cake roll on a serving plate, seam side down; position cut piece against side of cake roll to resemble a knot, using a little frosting to "glue" it in place. Spread remaining frosting over cake and knot. Score frosting with the tines of a fork to resemble tree bark. Chill cake before serving if frosting is soft. Garnish, if desired. Yield: 8 servings.

New Orleans-Style Dinner

Host friends for a casual soup supper. Transform your kitchen into a Crescent City diner with this native menu. Make the gumbo ahead, pick up some crusty bread at the bakery, and whip up dessert just before guests arrive.

Menu for 6

Shrimp and Sweet Potato Gumbo

French bread

Vanilla-Coconut Pears • Ice cream

Coffee bar

Shrimp and Sweet Potato Gumbo

Shrimp and Sweet Potato Gumbo

Roasted vegetables, smoked sausage, and smoked bacon add a unique depth of flavor to this gumbo. Forego the bacon in the recipe if you're in a pinch for time.

2 large onions, coarsely chopped
1 pound sweet potatoes, peeled and cut into 1" pieces
1 tablespoon olive oil
½ teaspoon salt
¼ teaspoon pepper
1 pound smoked sausage, sliced
6 smoked bacon slices, optional (we tested with Nueske's)
¼ cup vegetable oil
¼ cup all-purpose flour
2 celery ribs, chopped
1 green bell pepper, chopped
1 tablespoon minced garlic
3 cups water
1 (14½-ounce) can stewed tomatoes
1 (10¾-ounce) can tomato with roasted garlic and herbs soup, undiluted
1 (10¾-ounce) can chicken gumbo soup, undiluted
1 bay leaf
1 pound unpeeled, medium-size fresh shrimp, peeled, or 1 pound frozen peeled shrimp

Toss onion and sweet potato with 1 tablespoon olive oil; sprinkle with salt and pepper. Spread vegetables in a single layer in a shallow roasting pan or a 15" x 10" jelly-roll pan. Roast at 450° for 30 minutes, stirring twice.

Cook sausage in a large Dutch oven over medium heat until browned; remove sausage, and set aside.

Cook bacon in same pan over medium heat until crisp; remove bacon and drain on paper towels, reserving drippings in pan. Coarsely crumble bacon.

Add enough oil to drippings in pan to yield ¼ cup. Add flour and cook over medium heat, whisking constantly, until roux is peanut butter-colored (about 30 minutes). Add celery, green pepper, and garlic; cook 7 minutes or until vegetables are just tender. Stir in water and next 4 ingredients. Bring to a boil; cover, reduce heat, and simmer 20 minutes. Gently stir in roasted vegetables, sausage, and shrimp; cook 5 to 7 minutes or until shrimp turn pink. Discard bay leaf before serving.

To serve, ladle gumbo into individual bowls. Sprinkle each serving with bacon, if desired. Yield: 13½ cups.

Vanilla-Coconut Pears

Vanilla-Coconut Pears

Serve this warm fruit dessert as is or spoon it over praline ice cream (our recommendation), pound cake, waffles, or pancakes.

3 (15-ounce) cans chopped pears, undrained (we tested with Libby's)
2 tablespoons cornstarch
1 teaspoon vanilla extract
¼ teaspoon ground cinnamon
⅓ cup sugar
2 tablespoons bourbon
2 tablespoons butter or margarine
⅓ cup flaked coconut, toasted
¼ cup chopped pecans, toasted

Drain pears, reserving 1¼ cups liquid. Set pears aside. Combine ¼ cup reserved liquid with cornstarch, vanilla, and cinnamon, stirring until smooth.

Combine remaining 1 cup liquid with sugar, bourbon, and butter in a small saucepan; gradually stir in cornstarch mixture. Cook over low heat, stirring constantly, until butter melts and sauce is thickened.

Place pears in an ungreased 8" square baking dish. Pour sauce over pears; sprinkle with coconut and pecans.

Bake, uncovered, at 350° for 18 minutes or until bubbly. Serve warm. Yield: 6 servings.

Homestyle Holiday Supper

Have some friends over during the holidays for relaxing and feasting on this easy meal. Turkey pot pie and fudgy pudding cake—what could be more inviting?

Menu for 6

Green Chile-Turkey Pot Pie

Green salad • Lime-Marinated Tomatoes with Cilantro

Fudgy Mocha Melt • Coffee ice cream

Green Chile-Turkey Pot Pie

GREEN CHILE-TURKEY POT PIE

This one-dish pot pie is the ultimate in easy. You just spoon a cheesy biscuit topping over a turkey, bean, and green chile filling, and bake.

2 bunches green onions, chopped (about 1½ cups)
3 tablespoons vegetable oil
2 (4.5-ounce) cans chopped green chiles, undrained
1 (2.25-ounce) can sliced ripe olives, drained
¼ cup all-purpose flour
1½ teaspoons ground cumin
2 (16-ounce) cans pinto beans, rinsed and drained
1 (14-ounce) can chicken broth
2 cups chopped cooked turkey breast
1 cup all-purpose flour
1½ teaspoons baking powder
2 cups (8 ounces) shredded Mexican four-cheese blend (we tested with Sargento)
⅔ cup milk
1 large egg, lightly beaten

Sauté green onions in oil in a Dutch oven over medium heat 1 minute. Add green chiles and next 3 ingredients; cook 2 minutes, stirring constantly. Stir in beans and broth; bring to a boil. Reduce heat, and simmer, stirring constantly, 5 to 7 minutes or until mixture is thickened. Stir in turkey. Pour into a greased 13" x 9" baking dish.

Combine 1 cup flour and baking powder in a small bowl. Add cheese, milk, and egg, stirring just until blended. Spread biscuit topping over filling, leaving a 1" border around edge.

Bake, uncovered, at 375° for 30 minutes or until topping is golden and pot pie is bubbly. Yield: 6 servings.

LIME-MARINATED TOMATOES WITH CILANTRO

Here's an easy marinated tomato dish to pair with the pot pie. Plum tomatoes taste and look pretty good right through winter. If not, see the Note following the recipe.

6 plum tomatoes, cut into wedges
3 tablespoons vegetable or olive oil
1½ to 2 tablespoons fresh lime juice
1 tablespoon chopped fresh cilantro
½ teaspoon garlic salt
¼ teaspoon grated lime rind
⅛ teaspoon pepper

Place tomato wedges in a glass dish. Combine oil and remaining ingredients; stir well. Pour over tomato wedges. Cover and chill at least 1 hour. Yield: 6 servings.

Note: *If fresh tomatoes are not at their peak, substitute 2 (14½-ounce) cans tomato wedges, drained.*

FUDGY MOCHA MELT

If chocolate is the ultimate comfort food, then this dessert tops them all. It's a gooey pudding cake capped with coffee ice cream.

1 cup sugar
½ cup all-purpose flour
½ cup butter or margarine, melted
2 large eggs, lightly beaten
3 tablespoons cocoa
2 tablespoons finely chopped pecans
1 teaspoon instant coffee granules
½ teaspoon ground cinnamon
1 teaspoon vanilla extract
Coffee ice cream (we tested with Starbucks Java Chip)

Combine all ingredients except ice cream in a medium bowl, stirring until blended. Pour into a greased 8" baking dish. (Mixture will be shallow in dish.) Bake, uncovered, at 325° for 25 minutes.

To serve, spoon into dessert dishes. Top each serving with a scoop of ice cream. Serve immediately. Yield: 6 servings.

Fudgy Mocha Melt

THERE'S NO PLACE LIKE HOME

When it comes to finding the right ingredients for your holiday decorations, sometimes the best place to look is in your own cupboard.

Touches of Toile

Toile describes a printed pattern which depicts pastoral landscapes or historical scenes usually represented as one color over a lighter background. This centuries-old design remains fresh and stylish today—and especially in shades of red and green, it sets a warm holiday mood.

◀ Splendidly Styled

Toile fabric elevates the basic bottle bag to a new level of sophistication. Use a fabric paint pen to write the recipient's name on the ribbon for a personal touch. The bags are easily fashioned from fabric remnants. For instructions, see page 172.

Well-Appointed Wrappings ▶

Not exclusive to fabric, toile also appears in paper form—in this case, gift bags, wrapping paper, and tissue paper. Add a little drama to your packages at Christmas and continue this classic theme year-round.

Toile Toppers

Needing a small gift for a neighbor or co-worker? For a quick-and-easy present, buy ready-made jams and cap them with a fabric jar topper. Simply cut a small square from toile fabric remnants using pinking shears, place the square on the jar lid, and secure with cording or ribbon. To make a jar seem especially Christmassy, tuck a sprig of berries in the ribbon. ▼

Toile and Tea for Two

From the tablecovering to the tableware, toile offers enchanting party accessories for guests of any age. Although the napkins and tablecloth shown here are paper products, they could easily be made from square pieces of toile fabric. The plates pictured here are also paper, but a small transferware plate would make a stunning substitute.

Quick-as-a-Wink Table Topper

A square piece of fabric becomes an attractive table topper with the addition of fringe and cording. This no-sew version works equally well on a rectangular, round, or square table. The red toile fabric is festive enough to be an integral part of your holiday table setting yet elegant enough to use for year-round decorating.

To make the table topper, you'll need 1½ yards of 54-inch-wide fabric, 6 yards of bullion fringe, and 6 yards of decorative cording. Use hot glue and a hot-glue gun to apply dots of glue to the edge of the fabric, starting at the center of one side. Press the heading of the bullion fringe onto the dots of glue for several seconds to secure. At the corners of the fabric, fold the heading down at a 45-degree angle so that it will lie flat. Continue around the edges of the fabric until all sides are covered. (Be sure to keep your hands away from any exposed hot glue. If the glue comes through the fabric, press the heading down using a folded washcloth.)

Apply dots of hot glue to the heading of the bullion fringe. Press the cording onto the glue to secure. Cover the heading with cording on all sides of the fabric. Apply an extra dot of glue where the cording ends intersect.

Plate Upholstery

Make a set of these fancy plates to spruce up your home for the holidays—and keep them out all year! With inexpensive materials and handsome results, these plates make wonderful gifts.

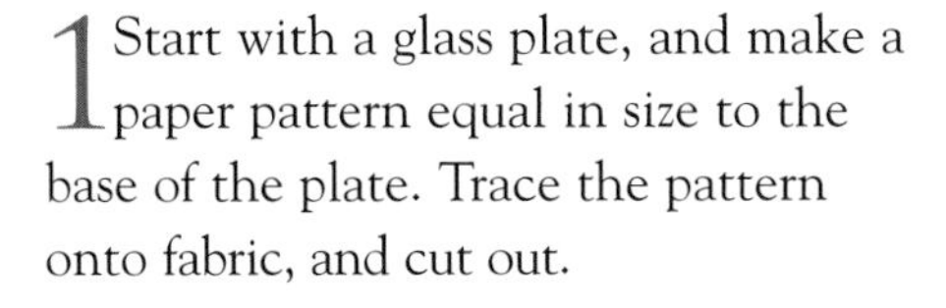

1 Start with a glass plate, and make a paper pattern equal in size to the base of the plate. Trace the pattern onto fabric, and cut out.

2 Using a foam brush, cover the front of the fabric circle with decoupage glue. Center the fabric on the underside of the plate and smooth out any wrinkles. Allow the glue to dry.

3 Apply glue to the underside of the plate. Cover the surface with a circle of coordinating fabric and smooth out any wrinkles. Trim excess fabric from the edge of the plate.

Merry
Christmas

Toile-Covered Door

A front door covered in toile fabric greets guests with a stylish holiday welcome. This twist on the traditional use of toile will surprise and delight visitors. Berry topiaries and a berry garland frame the door and add an accent of red to the entrance.

To make the door cover, measure the length and width of the door and add three inches on all sides. Using these dimensions, cut a rectangle from fabric. Use flat-headed thumbtacks to secure the fabric to the top of the door. Wrap the fabric around the sides of the door, pulling it taut so the fabric is evenly stretched. Use thumbtacks to secure the fabric to the sides and bottom of the door. Cut a circle opening to accommodate the doorknob.

To make the topiaries, you'll need two 12-inch diameter floral foam balls, holly and nandina berries, red carnations, ribbon, two wooden dowels painted black, Styrofoam, and two planters. Soak the floral foam balls in water until they are saturated. Cut the berry and flower stems so only a couple of inches remain. Insert berries and carnations into the floral foam balls to cover. Cut a block of Styrofoam to fit down into each of the planters. Center and insert a wooden dowel in each block of Styrofoam. Set each floral foam ball on top of each wooden dowel. Wire ribbon loops to floral picks and insert in the bottom of each floral foam ball to complete the topiaries. Place fresh greenery around the base of each topiary to hide the Styrofoam blocks.

Shined and Ready

Unwrap the silver and get a bright headstart on holiday decorating. Arrange platters, pitchers, candleholders—sterling, silverplate, pewter, or anything silver—to create glittery vignettes using accessories you have on hand.

▲ Sideboard Splendor

The glow of candlelight warms this setting which features a mix of silver candleholders, serving pieces, and frosty Christmas balls. White lilies and eucalyptus berries convey a lively air.

◀ A Cozy Combination

Blue-and-white china provides a homey backdrop for an eclectic collection of silver pieces. Using fruit, berries, and greenery clippings is an easy and inexpensive way to fill in the empty spaces with Christmas colors.

▲ Group Effort

A simple toiletry bottle, diminutive vase, and small-scale ornaments gain importance when grouped on a tray. The rosy red, gold, and purple hues festively glow against the cool silver tones.

◀ Sweet Cargo

Always consider including elements such as flowers, candy, and backyard clippings when planning your seasonal decorations. They are inexpensive, readily available, and offer a fresh component. Even tulips—an unexpected holiday flower—are available during the season at florist shops and many large grocery stores.

Sterling Silver Tips

Follow these maintenance ideas so your silver is always in mint condition.

- *Wash silver immediately after use in hot, soapy water. Rinse with hot water, and dry thoroughly.*
- *Sealed zip-top plastic bags are okay for storage, but don't wrap silver with plastic wrap or secure with rubber bands.*
- *Always use a brand-name silver polish. As the polishing cloth gets dirty, turn it over or replace with a new one to avoid scratches.*

Personal Favorites

If you have more than one of an item, then you have a collection. Though the pieces may reside in different rooms, during the holidays why not display them together as a group? Greenery, flowers, ribbons, and candles will make them a treasured feature of your Christmas decorating.

▲ For the Birds

Amass a village of birdhouses along a mantel to create a Christmas scene. Nest and stagger these aviaries according to height and color to bring interest and depth to the grouping. Add garland, fresh greenery, red ribbon, and a roaring fire to complete the holiday decor.

◀ Classic Ceramics

A color scheme can be the defining characteristic of a collection as with this blue-and-white porcelain grouping. While most of the pieces used aren't necessarily holiday decorations, a tiny nativity scene and an angel near the center give a sense of Christmas. Red velvet stockings, red ranunculus, and crimson candles accent the collection, bringing warmth to an otherwise cool arrangement.

Collection of Candlesticks

Ornate candlesticks are especially eye-catching when clustered in one setting. Arrange candlesticks and candles of varying heights and widths—there's no rule, just follow what's pleasing to your eye. Place clippings of pine, Fraser fir, seeded eucalyptus, heather, red pepperberries, holly, and nandina berries around the bases of the candles to embellish this festive arrangement.

To achieve a simple look, place a wired ring of greenery or red pepperberries around a candle. For a more elaborate display, set a small block of floral foam on top of the candlestick to use as a base. Set a candle on top of the floral foam block and insert cuttings into the foam to cover. Weave a mixed greenery garland around the bases of the candlesticks to unify the grouping.

Warm Glow of Copper

Fill a kitchen nook with copper pieces of all shapes and sizes. Pull pots out of the cabinets, molds off the wall, and kettles from the stove—anything copper goes. Holly, pinecones, and small branches of pine bring a holiday feel to the setting and soften the metallic tones. Red candles contribute flashes of color to the monochromatic arrangement while the reflection of the flames on the copperware offers a luminous effect.

A Snowy Show

Create a wintry shelf scene with a collection of snowmen, greenery clippings from the yard, and a sprinkling of faux snow. For extra glitter, add a few beaded snowflakes to the snowscape. Since snowmen are considered a winter decoration, this is one holiday display you can leave out long after New Year's Day.

A Variety of Vases

Allow your imagination to run free when choosing containers for your holiday arrangements. Here are a few suggestions that may surprise you.

◀ Cone Flowers

Painted terra-cotta pots are a fitting complement to these "planted" pinecones. Consider using a plain clay pot with a seasonal ribbon tied around the rim or with a simple handpainted border as an ideal choice for holding greenery clippings and berries.

▲ Cranberry Delight

Any clear container becomes a Christmassy creation when filled with cranberries. Add candles or a few flower stems, and it's worthy of being a dining room centerpiece. Tie it with a wide ribbon in honor of the holidays. For flowers, add water to the container.

◀ Not for Candles Only

Here, the globes of ornate candleholders do double duty as vases. Cranberries in water hold the flowers in place. Change the water every few days to keep the flowers fresh, and replace the cranberries, as needed.

Invited Inside ▶

Grab that urn that's been on the porch all year, and dress it for the holidays with a cheery carnation topiary. Stick twigs into a floral foam ball for the trunk, cover the ball with carnations, and secure the trunk in a floral foam block inside the urn. Embellish as desired with fruit, ribbons, and greenery.

Harvest Lights

This idea takes "candleholder" to a new level. Instead of a large pillar candle, fill the candle globes with an assortment of unshelled nuts. Place a votive candle securely in the center, and you have a decoration that will last from Thanksgiving through Christmas. Remember to keep the candle flame well above the nuts, and never leave burning candles unattended.

A Centerpiece in Seconds ▶

Any large glass bowl will work for this quick arrangement. Place a tall pillar candle in the center of the bowl, and surround it with pinecones and greenery. For a special touch, encircle the candle with tiny rosebuds.

ORNAMENTS EVERYWHERE

Traditionally thought of as decorations for the Christmas tree, ornaments dutifully take their places on branches from year to year. This season, showcase your favorites by displaying them in a different setting.

Lyrical and Lovely

Hung along a mantel, favorite ornaments have greater visibility and prominence than if they were hanging on a tree. A garland of greenery across the mantel is all that's needed for an elegant yet simple finishing touch. The ornaments shown here are based on the beloved Christmas carol, "The Twelve Days of Christmas," and represent a different day of the season and verse of the song.

Arrayed in Ribbons

Add luster to a light fixture by displaying favorite holiday ornaments in this eye-catching place. Coordinate ribbons with the ornaments to suit the decor. Carefully thread ornaments onto narrow widths of ribbon or onto clear fishing line. Suspend the ornaments from the chandelier's arms, varying the drop lengths for visual interest. Embellish the chandelier with wider ribbons, as desired.

Noel Nosegay

Transform pressed-tin cones from ornaments to Christmas tussie-mussies by filling them with ranunculus, hypericum, holly, greenery, and pinecones. Insert a small block of water-soaked floral foam into a heavy-duty plastic bag, and place it inside a cone. Insert cuttings into the floral foam. Tie a loop of ribbon to a floral pick using wire and insert the pick into the floral foam. Hang one cone on each arm of the chandelier, and invite guests to take one home as a remembrance of a fun evening.

◀ Decorated to Scale

Draping garland along a banister is not a new idea, but punctuating the greenery with oversize balls and cones offers a fresh alternative for decorating. While these large ornaments might overpower smaller ones on a tree, they are just the right size for this placement. Wire the cones to the garland, and fill them with red berries, greenery, holly, or even a ball. Secure the rest of the ornaments to garland using ribbon.

Metallic Magic ▶

Set apart especially fancy ornaments by hanging them from a candle sconce. Use long and varied lengths of gold and silver wired ribbon to attach ornaments to a gilded wall fixture. Tie bows around the candles to continue the glittery theme.

Sparkling Snowflakes

The enchanting nature of reflective ornaments is often hidden when they're hung on a Christmas tree. Consider displaying these prismatic beauties in a window for maximum light exposure. At night the crystalline ornaments stand out prominently against the dark backdrop, creating another spectacular effect.

Carefree Candlelight

Brightly twinkling candles are synonymous with Christmas celebrations, but keeping a cautious eye on open flames and dripping wax—especially tall, tipsy tapers—can be tedious. Here are ways to have the glow without the worry.

Tabletop Sparkle

Glass urns are a safe bet for creating a dramatic centerpiece as well as keeping candle flames out of harm's way. The ambience is heightened with a rich tapestry tablecloth, a shimmering gold table runner and ornaments, and jeweled wreaths encircling the bases of the urns.

ALL AGLOW
The warm radiance of this refined arrangement can be enjoyed without concern for wax drips, due to a large pillar candle and votives in tall holders.

Candle Style

With so many candle choices, it's easy to be creative. Here are a few ideas from our editors.

- *Use a silver tray to hold an arrangement of votives and pillars. Accent with greenery.*
- *Jelly jars make a great alternative to hurricane globes, especially for outdoors.*
- *Place a large pillar candle in an urn. Tuck in herbs around the bottom of the candle to offer complementary scents.*

Beaded Beauties ▲

These fancy bobeches (candle collars) are lovely enhancements to tall tapers. When the candles are lit, they also keep wax drips from falling on your tabletop.

Good Enough to Eat

Peppermint-striped floating candles form a festive candlelight centerpiece that is worry free. Group several sizes in a large bowl filled with water, and surround the bowl with single votives floating in water-filled votive holders. Fill tall jars with striped candies to enhance the theme. ▶

◀ Up and Away

A wrought-iron chandelier holds votive candles in deep glass cups, so you won't have to be quite as concerned about flames around the decorative greenery and garland.

IT'S THE THOUGHT

Gift giving takes on a delightful new dimension when you wrap presents with a dash of imagination. On the following pages, we show you how.

Special Presentations

Whether it's a treat baked in your oven or a treasure purchased at a favorite shop, a heartfelt gift is always well received—especially when its presented in a clever wrapping.

Sweet Containers

A paper cone filled with goodies recalls sweet treats from childhood. It's also a versatile way to contain food gifts such as the purchased biscotti and chocolate espresso beans pictured on these pages.

Using the pattern on page 172, cut out the cone from heavyweight paper. If you want to line your cone with a contrasting paper, cut one cone from each paper, and use double-sided tape to hold the pieces together. Punch two holes in the paper, as indicated on the pattern. Curl the edges of the cone toward the center, thread a ribbon through the holes, and tie. To keep the food fresh, be sure to place it in a plastic or cellophane bag before placing in the cone for gift giving.

Merry Christmas
Merry Christmas

Gift Cones

Paper cones are the answer to wrapping odd-shaped presents, and they can be reused again and again. To make a cone, cut a rectangle from construction paper. Roll the paper into a loose cone; trim the top with scissors to make a straight edge. Secure with double-sided tape. To line the cone with contrasting paper, cut one rectangle from each of two papers and hold them together with double-sided tape. For the handle, punch a hole on each side of the cone opening, thread a ribbon through the holes and knot the ribbon ends on the outside of the cone. Punch holes and lace ribbon along the top of the cone, as desired.

HAND-LABELED JARS

Yummy jams and jellies, whether homemade or store-bought, make tasty and beautiful hostess gifts. They're terrific for neighbors and teachers, as well. Make jars Christmassy with purchased sticker borders and labels; or create your own designs using adhesive-backed white paper, markers, and colored pencils. (To remove existing labels from jars, use a product designed to remove adhesives, which can be found at drugstores and hardware stores.)

▲ In Good Favor

Adorn your holiday table with these Christmas crackers, filling them with novelty items or candy. Set one at each plate as a place favor for guests. To make these party poppers, center a cardboard tube on one edge of a stack of several pieces of colored tissue paper. Secure the paper to the tube with tape. Roll the paper tightly around the tube, and secure it with double-sided tape. Tie ribbons around the tissue paper on each end of the tube. Cut a rectangle to size from wrapping paper or from a wallpaper border remnant, wrap it around the tube, and tape. A box full of these party favors also serves as a fun hostess gift.

◀ Puppy Treats

Don't forget man's best friend at holiday time. Fill a feeding bowl with pet toys, a brush, and dog biscuits. Wrap the bowl with cellophane, and tie it with a bow. You can paint a bowl with your own design at a specialty pottery shop, or buy a basic dish and fill it to overflowing with canine confections.

▲ "Hand"some Tags

Mitten gift tags make this the cutest package under the tree, hands down. Trace the mitten pattern on page 172 onto tracing paper, and transfer the shape onto thin colored foam or card stock. Cut out the tag and embellish it with a paint pen. Add festivity and flamboyance to the package with copious amounts of jingle bells and ribbons.

◀ Woodsy Wraps

Accent your Christmas packages with decorative acorns, berries, and raffia for striking good looks. Permanent woodland ornaments are shown, but nuts and berries from your backyard will work, as well. For wrapping several gifts into one, make a tower of different sized boxes and secure them with a wide ribbon, tying a bow at the top.

Clever Containers

Many everyday items can double as "boxes" for your holiday presents. Here are a couple of ideas.

- *Small enamel or galvanized buckets make terrific gift containers. Line with a bandanna, colorful napkin, or tissue paper. Tie a bow on the handle.*
- *Glue a ribbon around the rim of a terra-cotta pot. With the present inside, wrap the pot in cellophane and tie it at the top of the pot with the same ribbon used on the rim.*

From Bow to Beautiful

Instead of a stick-on bow, try this fresh approach to trimming your packages. Knot ribbon around sprigs of greenery and herbs for fragrant gift toppers. Small vine wreaths, found at crafts stores, are wonderful decorative elements that become a part of the gift, since they can be removed and hung up for the holidays.

▲Natural Resources

Give your packages a rustic look using an everyday household item—a brown lunch sack. Spruce up wrappings with greenery, pinecones, and ribbon. For gift bags, place the gift inside and fold down the top of the bag. Punch two holes at the top of the bag, and thread ribbon or even a small twig through the holes to hold it closed. Use hot glue to attach pinecones and greenery. To cover a small, flat gift, cut a sack open and wrap as if using wrapping paper.

Simply Spectacular▶

For added punch, place your gift in a colored paper bag. Small tags found at office supply stores become color-coordinated gift labels when decorated with paint pens and holiday stickers. Place the gift inside the bag, fold down the top, and punch two holes in the top center, about an inch apart. Thread ribbon through the holes, and slide the tags onto the ribbon ends. Tie the ribbon into a bow.

A FINE FINISH

A single bloom has enormous impact when used as a package topper. Place a flower stem and greenery sprigs in a water vial, and tuck the vial into the knot of the bow. A simple pinecone makes a neat embellishment, too. Just tie in place with ribbon or raffia, as shown here.

HOLIDAY RECIPES

Savor the magic of the season with our grand selection of cookies, slow cooker sensations, and Southern Living *classics.*

Southern Living Classics

What makes a recipe classic? It's food that has instant success at the family table. It's that certain dish your family will remember and request from year to year. We share a quintet of Christmas classics on the following pages.

Florentine Artichoke Dip

For twenty-two years we've tested and tasted holiday recipes for this book to help make your celebrations more memorable. I've personally spearheaded recipe selection for the last eight years, and as a result, many friends and coworkers come to me and ask for holiday recipe recommendations. It's never easy to offer only a few ideas, but I'd like to share five of my personal favorites with you. I hope you enjoy them as much as I do year after year. *Julie Gunter, Foods Editor*

Florentine Artichoke Dip

Spinach, artichoke hearts, and two cheeses blend beautifully in this hot appetizer. Roasted garlic bagel chips were our favorite dippers.

1 (10-ounce) package frozen chopped spinach, thawed
2 (6½-ounce) jars marinated artichoke hearts, drained and chopped
1½ (8-ounce) packages cream cheese, softened
1 cup freshly shredded Parmesan cheese
½ cup mayonnaise
3 large garlic cloves, pressed
2 tablespoons lemon juice
1½ cups French breadcrumbs (homemade) (see Note)
2 tablespoons butter or margarine, melted

Drain spinach; press between layers of paper towels to remove excess moisture.

Combine spinach, artichoke hearts, and next 5 ingredients in a bowl, stirring well. Spoon into a lightly greased 11" x 7" baking dish. Combine breadcrumbs and butter; sprinkle over spinach mixture.

Bake, uncovered, at 375° for 25 minutes. Serve with assorted crackers, bagel chips, or breadsticks. Yield: 4 cups.

Note: *To get 1½ cups French breadcrumbs, tear off a piece of a baguette. Pulse in a food processor until coarse crumbs form. Measure crumbs, tear off another chunk, and repeat procedure until you get 1½ cups.*

Roasted Sweet Potato Salad

Tossed in a rosemary-honey vinaigrette, these slightly charred potatoes come alive with flavor.

4 large sweet potatoes, peeled and cubed
2 tablespoons olive oil, divided
¼ cup honey
3 tablespoons white wine vinegar
2 tablespoons chopped fresh rosemary
½ teaspoon salt
½ teaspoon freshly ground pepper
2 garlic cloves, minced
Garnish: fresh rosemary sprig

Coat a large roasting pan with cooking spray; toss together potato and 1 tablespoon oil in pan.

Bake, uncovered, at 450° for 35 to 45 minutes or until potato is tender and roasted, stirring after 20 minutes.

Whisk together remaining 1 tablespoon oil, honey, and next 5 ingredients. Transfer warm potato to a large serving bowl; add dressing, and toss gently. Cool. Garnish, if desired. Yield: 6 to 8 servings.

Note: *Serve this salad chilled or at room temperature. Refrigerate it overnight to blend flavors, if desired.*

Roasted Sweet Potato Salad

Leslie's Favorite Chicken-and-Wild Rice Casserole

This is one of those creamy, cheesy chicken casseroles. Perfect for a big family get-together, it feeds a crowd. You can make and freeze the casserole ahead, or make two small casseroles.

2 (6.2-ounce) packages fast-cooking long-grain and wild rice mix
1/4 cup butter or margarine
4 celery ribs, chopped
2 medium onions, chopped
2 (8-ounce) cans sliced water chestnuts, drained
5 cups chopped cooked chicken
4 cups (1 pound) shredded Cheddar cheese, divided
2 (10 3/4-ounce) cans cream of mushroom soup, undiluted
2 (8-ounce) containers sour cream
1 cup milk
1/2 teaspoon salt
1/2 teaspoon pepper
1/2 cup soft breadcrumbs (homemade)
1 (2.25-ounce) package sliced almonds, toasted

Prepare rice mixes according to package directions.

Melt butter in a large skillet over medium heat; add celery and onion. Sauté 10 minutes or until tender. Stir in water chestnuts, rice, chicken, 3 cups cheese, and next 5 ingredients.

Spoon mixture into a lightly greased 15" x 10" baking dish or a 4-quart baking dish. Top casserole with breadcrumbs. Bake at 350° for 35 minutes. Sprinkle with remaining 1 cup cheese and almonds; bake 5 more minutes. Yield: 10 to 12 servings.

Note: *You can divide this casserole evenly between 2 (11" x 7") baking dishes. Bake as directed above or freeze casserole up to 1 month. Remove from freezer, and let stand at room temperature 1 hour. Bake, covered, at 350° for 30 minutes. Uncover casserole, and bake 55 more minutes. Sprinkle with remaining 1 cup cheese and almonds, and bake 5 more minutes.*

Leslie Flemister, Dunwoody, Georgia

Leslie's Favorite Chicken-and-Wild Rice Casserole

Bourbon-Chocolate Pecan Pie

BOURBON-CHOCOLATE PECAN PIE

This decadent chocolate pecan pie is every bit as sinful if you choose to leave out the bourbon. And the pie is so rich, it doesn't need a garnish. On the other hand, see our note below for the ultimate chocolate blowout.

½ (15-ounce) package refrigerated piecrusts
4 large eggs
1 cup light corn syrup
6 tablespoons butter or margarine, melted
½ cup sugar
¼ cup firmly packed light brown sugar
3 tablespoons bourbon (optional)
1 tablespoon all-purpose flour
1 tablespoon vanilla extract
1 cup coarsely chopped pecans
1 cup (6 ounces) semisweet chocolate morsels, melted

Fit piecrust into a lightly greased 9" pieplate according to package directions, being careful to press together any cracks. Fold edges under, and crimp.

Whisk together eggs and next 7 ingredients until blended; stir in pecans and melted chocolate. Pour filling into piecrust.

Bake on lowest oven rack at 350° for 1 hour or until set, shielding pie with aluminum foil after 20 minutes. Cool completely on a wire rack. Yield: 1 (9") pie.

Note: *If you're one who likes a topping on every dessert, then you'll be inspired by the cover of this book. For a chocolate blowout, add these toppings to the pie: whipped cream, chocolate shavings, and fudge sauce.*

NEW ORLEANS DOUBLE-CHOCOLATE CHRISTMAS PRALINE-FUDGE CAKE

1 cup butter or margarine
¼ cup cocoa
1 cup water
½ cup buttermilk
2 large eggs
1 teaspoon baking soda
1 teaspoon vanilla extract
2 cups sugar
2 cups all-purpose flour
½ teaspoon salt
Chocolate Ganache
Praline Frosting
Garnish: chopped pecans

Cook first 3 ingredients in a saucepan over low heat, stirring constantly, until butter melts and mixture is smooth; remove from heat. Cool.

Beat buttermilk, 2 eggs, baking soda, and vanilla at medium speed with an electric mixer until smooth. Add butter mixture to buttermilk mixture, beating until blended. Combine sugar, flour, and salt; gradually add to buttermilk mixture, beating until blended. (Batter will be thin.)

Coat 3 (8") round cakepans with cooking spray; line with wax paper. Pour batter evenly into pans. Bake at 350° for 22 to 24 minutes or until set. Cool in pans on wire racks 10 minutes. Remove from pans, and cool layers completely.

Spread about ½ cup ganache between cake layers; spread remainder on sides of cake. Chill cake ½ hour. Pour frosting slowly over center of cake, spreading to edges, allowing some frosting to run over sides. Freeze, if desired; thaw at room temperature 4 to 6 hours. Garnish, if desired. Yield: 1 (8") layer cake.

CHOCOLATE GANACHE

2 cups (12 ounces) semisweet chocolate morsels
⅓ cup whipping cream
¼ cup butter or margarine, cut into pieces

Microwave chocolate morsels and cream in a glass bowl at MEDIUM (50% power) 2 to 3 minutes or until morsels are melted. Whisk until smooth. Gradually add butter, whisking until smooth. Cool, whisking often, 15 to 20 minutes or until spreading consistency. Yield: about 2 cups.

PRALINE FROSTING

Do not prepare this candylike frosting ahead because it'll harden very quickly.

¼ cup butter or margarine
1 cup firmly packed light brown sugar
⅓ cup whipping cream
1 cup powdered sugar
1 teaspoon vanilla extract
1 cup chopped pecans, toasted

Bring first 3 ingredients to a boil in a 2-quart saucepan over medium heat, stirring often; boil 1 minute. Remove from heat, and whisk in powdered sugar and vanilla until smooth. Add toasted pecans, stirring gently 2 to 5 minutes or until frosting begins to cool and thicken slightly. Pour immediately over cake. Yield: about 1¾ cups.

Note: *You can use 3 (9") round cakepans for this recipe. Bake layers at 350° for 18 to 22 minutes.*

Slow and Easy Christmas Cooking

Slow cookers have many timesaving benefits, and during the busy days of Christmas, you'll love these slow cooker entrées that get you out of the kitchen and ready to spend time with loved ones.

Slow Cooker Turkey and Dressing

Slow Cooker Turkey and Dressing

Turkey and dressing has never been so simple. See our series of photos below. You may never go back to roasting the bird after you try this easy version.

- 1 (8-ounce) package herb-seasoned stuffing mix (we tested with Pepperidge Farm)
- 1 onion, chopped
- 2 celery ribs, chopped
- 1 cup dried cranberries
- ¾ cup chicken broth
- 3 tablespoons butter or margarine, melted
- 1 (3-pound) frozen boneless turkey breast, thawed
- ¼ teaspoon salt
- ½ teaspoon pepper
- ¼ teaspoon dried thyme
- 1 (0.88-ounce) package turkey gravy mix

Coat inside of a 4-quart electric slow cooker with cooking spray. Add stuffing mix, onion, celery, and cranberries. Combine broth and melted butter. Pour over stuffing, and stir gently.

Remove string from turkey breast. Rinse turkey breast. Place turkey in slow cooker on top of stuffing. Combine salt, pepper, and thyme; sprinkle over turkey. Cover and cook on HIGH 1 hour. Reduce to LOW, and cook 5 to 6 hours or until a meat thermometer inserted in turkey registers 170°.

Remove turkey to a serving platter. Stir stuffing gently in slow cooker; cover and let stand 3 to 4 minutes. Prepare gravy. Spoon stuffing around turkey on platter. Yield: 5 to 6 servings.

Note: *Some turkey breasts come with a gravy packet; some don't. We liked the flavor and color of gravy using a (0.88-ounce) package of turkey gravy mix (we tested with French's).*

Beef Brisket with Shiitake Mushrooms and Red Wine Sauce

The slow cooker does its best work as it simmers beef brisket to extreme tenderness with mushrooms and onions in red wine.

- 1 (3-pound) boneless beef brisket
- ¾ teaspoon salt, divided
- ¾ teaspoons freshly ground pepper, divided
- 2 tablespoons vegetable oil
- 2 small onions, thinly sliced
- ½ pound fresh shiitake mushrooms, stems removed
- ½ cup dry red wine
- ½ cup beef consommé
- ¼ cup ketchup
- 1 teaspoon prepared horseradish
- 1 large garlic clove, minced
- 2 tablespoons all-purpose flour
- 2 tablespoons water

Trim excess fat from brisket. Rub brisket with ½ teaspoon salt and ½ teaspoon pepper. Brown brisket on both sides in hot oil in a large skillet over medium-high heat.

Place half of onion slices in bottom of a 6-quart electric slow cooker. Top with mushrooms. Combine red wine and next 4 ingredients; stir well. Drizzle half of red wine mixture over mushrooms; top with brisket. Place remaining half of onion slices on top of brisket. Drizzle with remaining red wine mixture. Cover and cook on HIGH 1 hour. Reduce to LOW, and cook 9 hours.

Remove meat to a serving platter; keep warm. Remove vegetables with a slotted spoon; set aside. Reserve 2 cups liquid in slow cooker.

Stir together flour and water until smooth; stir into reserved liquid. Cover and cook on HIGH 15 to 20 minutes. Add vegetables, remaining ¼ teaspoon salt, and remaining ¼ teaspoon pepper; stir well. Serve wine sauce over brisket. Yield: 6 to 8 servings.

1. Add stuffing mix to greased slow cooker.

2. Pour broth and melted butter over stuffing ingredients, and stir.

3. Place turkey over stuffing. Sprinkle with seasonings; cover and cook.

Nutty Snack Mix

NUTTY SNACK MIX

Test Kitchens Director Elizabeth Luckett stirs up this snack mix every year and passes it out to all her neighbors and friends. She likes the recipe because it makes a lot and uses entire packages of cereals and crackers.

- 1 (16-ounce) package crisp wheat cereal squares (we tested with Wheat Chex)
- 1 (13½-ounce) package baked snack crackers (we tested with Cheese Nips)
- 1 (12-ounce) package corn-and-rice cereal (we tested with Crispix)
- 1 (10-ounce) package toasted oat O-shaped cereal (we tested with Cheerios)
- 6 cups small pretzel twists
- 1 pound pecan halves
- 1 (16-ounce) can cocktail peanuts
- 2½ cups butter or margarine, melted
- ¼ cup Worcestershire sauce
- 2 tablespoons garlic powder
- 1½ tablespoons onion salt
- 1½ tablespoons celery salt
- ½ teaspoon ground red pepper

Combine first 7 ingredients in a large roasting pan. Stir together butter and remaining 5 ingredients; pour over cereal mixture, and toss well.

Cover and bake at 225° for 1 hour. Uncover and bake 1 more hour, stirring occasionally. Cool completely. Store in airtight containers. Yield: 42 cups.

Note: *We baked the snack mix in a 16" x 12" roasting pan and the pan was full. You can use 2 smaller roasting pans, but keep in mind the baking time will be less.*

Sausage and Pecan Baked Apples

These sausage-stuffed side dish apples could almost be dessert, thanks to the delicious drizzle of maple-orange syrup.

- 1 pound ground pork sausage
- 1 cup maple syrup, divided
- ¾ cup coarsely chopped pecans
- ½ cup orange marmalade, divided
- ¼ cup raisins
- 3 tablespoons water
- 8 Braeburn apples or other cooking apples
- 1 tablespoon lemon juice

Brown sausage in a large skillet, stirring until it crumbles and is no longer pink; drain well on paper towels.

Combine sausage, ½ cup maple syrup, pecans, ¼ cup orange marmalade, and raisins in a large bowl; toss well, and set aside.

Stir together remaining ½ cup syrup, remaining ¼ cup marmalade, and 3 tablespoons water in a small bowl.

Core apples, starting at stem end, to, but not through, opposite end. Enlarge opening to 1". Peel 1" around tops of apples. Brush cut part of apples with lemon juice.

Divide sausage mixture evenly between each apple, packing firmly and mounding lightly on top. Place filled apples in an ungreased 13" x 9" baking dish. Spoon about 1 tablespoon marmalade mixture over each apple. Cover and bake at 350° for 40 minutes; drizzle evenly with remaining marmalade mixture. Bake, covered, 20 to 25 more minutes or until apples are just tender. Uncover and bake 10 more minutes. Cool in dish on a wire rack 5 minutes. Serve warm, drizzling apples with remaining syrup in dish. Yield: 8 servings.

Note: *We found that Braeburn apples held their shape best during baking.*

Sausage and Pecan Baked Apples

White Chocolate, Peanut, and Caramel Candy Cookies

White Chocolate, Peanut, and Caramel Candy Cookies

White chocolate, peanuts, and chocolate-covered caramel candies give these drop cookies dynamite flavor.

1 cup butter or margarine, softened
1 cup sugar
1 cup firmly packed light brown sugar
2 large eggs
1 teaspoon vanilla extract
2½ cups uncooked regular oats
2 cups all-purpose flour
1 teaspoon baking powder
½ teaspoon baking soda
½ teaspoon salt
3 (1.91-ounce) packages chocolate-covered caramel candies, chilled and chopped (we tested with Rolo)
2 (4-ounce) white chocolate bars, chopped (we tested with Ghirardelli)
1½ cups unsalted peanuts, chopped

Beat butter at medium speed with an electric mixer until creamy; add sugars, beating well. Add eggs and vanilla, beating until blended.

Process oats in a blender or food processor until finely ground. Combine oats, flour, and next 3 ingredients; add to butter mixture, beating well. Stir in chopped candy, white chocolate, and peanuts.

Shape dough into 1½" balls, and place on parchment paper-lined baking sheets. Bake at 375° for 10 minutes or until lightly browned. Cool 1 minute on baking sheets. Remove to wire racks to cool. Yield: 6 dozen.

Note: *Find chocolate-covered caramel candies at your local drug store on the candy aisle. The candies may make the cookies stick slightly to the baking sheet. That's why we recommend baking these on parchment paper.*

Chocolate-Peanut Tart

Chocolate-Peanut Tart

A chocolate, chesslike filling snuggles peanuts in place in this scrumptious dessert. Use pecans if you'd rather.

½ (15-ounce) package refrigerated piecrusts
1¼ cups sugar
½ cup water
⅔ cup heavy whipping cream, warmed
3 tablespoons bourbon
¼ cup butter or margarine, melted
1 large egg, lightly beaten
1¼ cups roasted unsalted peanuts
¾ cup (4.5 ounces) semisweet chocolate morsels
Vanilla ice cream or unsweetened whipped cream (optional)

Fit piecrust into a greased 9" tart pan with a removable bottom.

Combine sugar and water in a medium saucepan; bring to a boil, stirring constantly until sugar dissolves. Reduce heat to medium-high, and boil, without stirring, 7 to 8 minutes or until syrup is golden, swirling pan occasionally. (Wash down sides of pan with water, using a pastry brush, if sugar crystals form on sides.)

Remove from heat, and gradually stir in warm cream and bourbon (mixture will bubble up). Cool completely (about 35 minutes).

Add butter and egg, stirring until smooth. Stir in peanuts and chocolate morsels. Pour mixture into prepared crust.

Bake at 375° for 36 to 38 minutes. Cool completely in pan on a wire rack. If desired, serve with vanilla ice cream or unsweetened whipped cream. Yield: 1 (9") tart.

Pumpkin Custards with Crunchy Pecan Topping

The smooth texture of these custards resembles a cross between pumpkin pie and pudding. The crunchy topping is the perfect complement. There'll be some leftover for you to sprinkle over ice cream or enjoy as a snack.

1 (15-ounce) can pumpkin
¾ cup heavy whipping cream
½ cup sugar
½ cup firmly packed dark brown sugar
½ teaspoon salt
½ teaspoon grated orange rind
¼ teaspoon freshly grated nutmeg
¼ teaspoon ground cinnamon
⅛ teaspoon ground ginger
⅛ teaspoon ground cloves
2 large eggs, lightly beaten
¼ cup butter or margarine
1 cup chopped pecans
½ cup sugar

Stir together first 11 ingredients in a large bowl.

Pour mixture evenly into 8 lightly greased 4-ounce ramekins or custard cups. Place in a large roasting pan; add hot water to pan to depth of 1". Bake, uncovered, at 325° for 55 minutes.

Pumpkin Custards with Crunchy Pecan Topping

Meanwhile, melt butter in a large skillet over medium heat; add pecans and ½ cup sugar. Cook, stirring constantly, 6 minutes or until sugar is dissolved and mixture is just golden brown. Pour onto a parchment paper-lined pan, spreading evenly. Cool completely; break into small pieces, and set aside.

Remove ramekins from water; cool slightly on wire racks. Cover and chill up to 24 hours, if desired.

To serve, top each custard with 1½ tablespoons pecan topping. Yield: 8 servings.

Pear, Roquefort, and Caramelized Onion Galette

A galette *is a rustic French tart whose filling is typically exposed to tempt you into the first bite. This nutty pear galette can serve as an appetizer, side dish, or dessert with a glass of wine.*

2 large sweet onions, thinly sliced (about 2 pounds)
1 tablespoon butter or margarine, melted
¼ teaspoon salt
¼ teaspoon freshly ground pepper
½ (15-ounce) package refrigerated piecrusts
2 firm Bosc pears, peeled and thinly sliced
1 tablespoon all-purpose flour
½ cup coarsely chopped pecans
3 ounces crumbled Roquefort cheese
1 large egg, lightly beaten

Cook onion in butter in a large skillet over medium-low heat, 30 to 35 minutes or until onion is caramelized, stirring often. Stir in salt and pepper; set aside.

Unfold piecrust and roll into a 14" circle on a lightly floured surface. Transfer to a parchment paper-lined baking sheet.

Combine pear slices and flour; toss gently to coat.

Spread three-fourths of onion over piecrust, leaving a 4" border around edges. Arrange pear slices over onion; top with remaining onion, pecans, and cheese. Fold over 4" borders of dough, pressing gently to seal. Brush dough with beaten egg.

Bake at 425° for 24 to 25 minutes or until golden, shielding with aluminum foil, if necessary, to prevent excessive browning. Cool on baking sheet on a wire rack 5 minutes. Serve warm, or cool to room temperature on wire rack. Yield: 8 to 10 servings.

Pear, Roquefort, and Caramelized Onion Galette

STELLAR SHORTBREAD

Buttery, sandy-textured shortbread is about as simple as a Christmas cookie can get. We bring you this familiar favorite plus several scrumptious variations, all great for nibbling or holiday gift-giving.

Basic Shortbread

BASIC SHORTBREAD

Shortbread is made from a few basic ingredients, and the results are sensational. The key to success with this thick shortbread is baking it slowly so that it doesn't brown.

- 1 cup butter, softened
- ½ cup sugar
- ¼ teaspoon vanilla extract
- 2¼ cups unbleached all-purpose flour (we tested with King Arthur)
- ⅛ teaspoon salt

Beat butter at medium speed with an electric mixer until creamy; gradually add sugar, beating well. Stir in vanilla.

Combine flour and salt; gradually add to butter mixture, beating at low speed until blended.

Roll dough to ½" thickness on a lightly floured surface. Cut with a 2½" round cutter or Christmas cookie cutter. Place 2" apart on an ungreased baking sheet.

Bake at 275° for 50 minutes. Cool 2 minutes on baking sheet. Remove to a wire rack to cool. Yield: 1 dozen.

Note: *Unbleached flour is the best-quality, freshest flour for baking and is particularly good in simple recipes like shortbread. Other kinds of all-purpose flour work fine in this recipe, too.*

Shortbread Stack

To create the pyramid of Basic Shortbread, you'll need a graduated set of round cookie cutters. Just roll and stamp out dough using each of the different-sized cutters. We used a 1½" cutter for our smallest cookie and a 4¼" cutter for the largest. And believe it or not, all the different sizes baked at 275° about the same length of time, from 50 to 55 minutes.

Cookies 'n' Cream Shortbread

COOKIES 'N' CREAM SHORTBREAD

Everybody's favorite sandwich cookie appears where you'd least expect it, crushed and stirred into another cookie.

- 1 cup butter, softened
- ½ cup sugar
- ¼ teaspoon vanilla extract
- 2¼ cups all-purpose flour
- ⅛ teaspoon salt
- 14 chocolate sandwich cookies, coarsely crumbled (1½ cups) (we tested with Oreos)

Beat butter at medium speed with an electric mixer until creamy; gradually add sugar, beating well. Stir in vanilla.

Combine flour and salt; gradually add to butter mixture, beating at low speed until blended. Stir in cookie crumbs. (The more you blend the cookie crumbs into the dough, the darker it gets. If you want a lightly marbled shortbread, barely stir crumbs in; if you want a more chocolaty cookie, stir longer.)

Roll dough to ½" thickness on a lightly floured surface. Cut with a 2½" round cutter or Christmas cookie cutter. Place 2" apart on ungreased baking sheets.

Bake at 275° for 48 minutes or until bottoms barely begin to brown. Cool 2 minutes on baking sheets. Remove to wire racks to cool. Yield: about 1½ dozen.

Chewy Coffee-Toffee Shortbread

Chewy Coffee-Toffee Shortbread

Toffee bits give this golden shortbread its slightly chewy texture. This cookie is particularly nice dipped in a cup of coffee.

1 cup butter, softened
½ cup firmly packed light brown sugar
1 tablespoon instant espresso powder (we tested with Café Bustelo)
1 tablespoon hot water
2¼ cups all-purpose flour
⅛ teaspoon salt
½ cup almond toffee bits (we tested with Hershey's)

Beat butter at medium speed with an electric mixer until creamy; gradually add sugar, beating well. Stir together espresso powder and water. Add to butter mixture, stirring well.

Combine flour and salt; gradually add to butter mixture, beating at low speed until blended. Stir in toffee bits. Cover and chill dough 30 minutes.

Roll dough to ½" thickness on a lightly floured surface. Cut with a 2½" round cutter or Christmas cookie cutter. Place 2" apart on ungreased baking sheets.

Bake at 275° for 50 minutes. Cool 2 minutes on baking sheets. Remove to wire racks to cool. Yield: 16 cookies.

Note: *If you can't find almond toffee bits in the supermarket, substitute ½ cup finely crushed Skor candy bars or crushed Werther's Original candies.*

Almond Shortbread

Ground natural almonds and almond extract pump up this shortbread with nutty goodness.

⅔ cup natural almonds, toasted (see Note)
1 cup butter, softened
½ cup sugar
1 teaspoon almond extract
2¼ cups all-purpose flour
⅛ teaspoon salt

Place almonds in a food processor; process until finely ground. Set aside.

Beat butter at medium speed with an electric mixer until creamy; gradually add sugar, beating well. Stir in almond extract.

Combine ground almonds, flour, and salt; gradually add to butter mixture, beating at low speed until blended.

Roll dough to ½" thickness on a lightly floured surface. Cut with a 2½" round cutter or Christmas cookie cutter. Place 2" apart on ungreased baking sheets.

Bake at 275° for 45 minutes. Cool 2 minutes on baking sheets. Remove to wire racks to cool. Yield: 17 cookies.

Note: *Toast natural almonds on a baking sheet at 350° for 6 to 8 minutes or until they smell fragrant. Then cool and grind almonds in a food processor until almost a powder consistency. We found that leaving the skins on the nuts adds a pleasing speckled appearance and rich flavor to the shortbread.*

Almond Shortbread

Peanut Butter-Chocolate Chip Shortbread

Peanut Butter Shortbread

Peanut Butter Shortbread

Creamy peanut butter adds a tasty new dimension to this butter cookie.

- 3/4 cup butter, softened
- 1/2 cup creamy peanut butter
- 1/2 cup firmly packed light brown sugar
- 1/4 teaspoon vanilla extract
- 2 1/4 cups all-purpose flour
- 1/4 teaspoon salt

Beat butter and peanut butter at medium speed with an electric mixer until creamy; gradually add sugar, beating well. Stir in vanilla.

Combine flour and salt; gradually add to butter mixture, beating at low speed until blended.

Roll dough to 1/2" thickness on a lightly floured surface. Cut with a 2 1/2" round cutter or Christmas cookie cutter. Place 2" apart on ungreased baking sheets.

Bake at 275° for 45 minutes. Cool 2 minutes on baking sheets. Remove to wire racks to cool. Yield: 15 cookies.

Peanut Butter-Chocolate Chip Shortbread: Stir 1/2 cup semisweet chocolate mini-morsels into the dough before rolling, cutting, and baking.

Give stacks of five flavors of shortbread as gifts. Wrap each stack in heavy-duty plastic wrap, tie with ribbon, and include a listing of the five flavors.

Aunt Neal's
Tea Cakes
Thumbprints
Fudgy-Peppermint
Gretchen's Mocha-Chocolate Chip Biscotti
Peanut Butter Cookies
Triple-Nut Chocolate Clover Cookies
-Kathleen
Salted Peanut Chews
-Gayle

Our Staff Cookie Swap

Who's most likely to have the best, most sinful holiday cookie collection? Who else, but our very own Oxmoor House Test Kitchens staff. Every year, each staff member bakes a family-favorite confection, packages enough cookies so everyone gets a sampling, makes cookie labels, and heads proudly to the party. Don't miss the anecdote included just below each recipe title.

Easy Oatmeal-Chocolate Chip Cookies

I nicknamed these "Trev" cookies because my husband Trevor likes them so much. Before that they were "Marsha" cookies, named for a friend who gave me the recipe. It's an easy recipe because you don't have to cream butter or shortening; you just dump and stir ingredients in a big bowl. — *Jan Smith*

2 cups all-purpose flour
1 teaspoon baking soda
½ teaspoon baking powder
½ teaspoon salt
2 cups uncooked quick-cooking oats
1 cup sugar
1 cup firmly packed light brown sugar
1 cup chopped pecans
1 cup (6 ounces) semisweet chocolate morsels
1 cup vegetable oil
2 large eggs, beaten
1 teaspoon vanilla extract

Stir together first 9 ingredients in a large bowl. Add oil, eggs, and vanilla; stir well.

Shape mixture into 1" balls. (Dough will be crumbly.) Place balls on ungreased baking sheets. Bake at 350° for 10 minutes or until golden. Let cool on baking sheets 1 minute. Remove to wire racks to cool. Yield: 6 dozen.

Tailored Tags

Homemade tags contribute to the personal touch of cookie swaps.

Aunt Neal's Old-Fashioned Tea Cakes

These delicious tea cakes were made by Aunt Cornelia ("Neal") on special occasions and holidays, using homemade hand-churned butter and eggs she gathered from the henhouse. This southern Georgia version dates back to the turn of the twentieth century. Ana Kelly

1 cup butter, softened
1 cup sugar
1 large egg, lightly beaten
1 teaspoon vanilla extract
3 cups all-purpose flour
1 teaspoon baking powder
½ teaspoon baking soda
½ teaspoon salt
½ cup milk
Sparkling white sugar

Beat butter at medium speed with an electric mixer until creamy; gradually add 1 cup sugar, beating well. Add egg and vanilla; beat well. Combine flour and next 3 ingredients; add to butter mixture alternately with milk, beginning and ending with flour mixture. Mix at low speed after each addition just until blended. Shape dough into 2 discs. Wrap in wax paper, and chill at least 1 hour.

Roll each disc to ¼" thickness on a floured surface. Cut with a 3½" round cutter; place 1" apart on lightly greased baking sheets. Sprinkle with sparkling sugar. Bake at 400° for 7 to 8 minutes or until edges are lightly browned. Cool 1 minute on baking sheets; remove to wire racks to cool. Yield: 2 dozen.

Raspberry-Almond Thumbprints

Cover the jam centers of these cookies with a circle of wax paper before dusting them with powdered sugar. This little trick keeps the jam a vibrant red color in these family-favorite cookies. Jennifer Cofield

½ cup butter or margarine, softened
½ cup sugar
1 large egg, separated
1 teaspoon vanilla extract
1¼ cups all-purpose flour
⅔ cup sliced blanched almonds, coarsely chopped
2 tablespoons seedless raspberry jam
Sifted powdered sugar

Beat butter at medium speed with an electric mixer until creamy; gradually add sugar, beating well. Add egg yolk and vanilla, beating until blended. Stir in flour. (Dough will be crumbly but easily presses together.) Form dough into a ball; cover and chill 3 hours.

Let dough stand at room temperature 5 minutes. Shape into 24 (1") balls. Lightly beat egg white. Dip each ball into egg white; roll in almonds, pressing firmly. Place balls 1" apart on lightly greased baking sheets. Make an indentation with your thumb in center of each cookie. Fill with about ¼ teaspoon raspberry jam.

Bake at 350° for 15 to 17 minutes or until lightly browned. Remove to wire racks to cool. Cut a small circle out of wax paper to fit over jam center. Place wax paper on jam, and dust with powdered sugar; remove wax paper circle. Repeat procedure with remaining cookies and powdered sugar. Yield: 2 dozen.

Dew Berry's Fruitcake Cookies

My family always stocked up on pecans each fall so we'd be ready for the holiday baking season. Dr. Berry was a family friend and veterinarian, and his wife, Dew, was our source for great pecans. She shared this nutty fruitcake cookie with my mom thirty-five years ago, and it's been a holiday favorite ever since. — *Julie Christopher*

1½ pounds raisins (4 cups)
⅓ cup bourbon
¾ cup butter, softened
1 cup firmly packed light brown sugar
¼ cup loosely packed orange zest
4 large eggs
1 teaspoon baking soda
2 tablespoons milk
3 cups all-purpose flour
1 teaspoon ground cinnamon
1 teaspoon ground nutmeg
1½ teaspoons salt
½ cup bourbon
5 cups pecans, chopped
1 pound candied pineapple, chopped (2½ cups)
½ pound red candied cherries, chopped (about 1 cup)
½ pound green candied cherries, chopped (about 1 cup)

Combine raisins and ⅓ cup bourbon in a very large bowl; toss. Set aside.

Beat butter at medium speed with an electric mixer until creamy; gradually add brown sugar, and beat until fluffy. Add orange zest and eggs, beating well. Dissolve baking soda in milk; stir into butter mixture. Combine flour and next 3 ingredients; add to butter mixture, stirring well. Stir in ½ cup bourbon.

Add pecans and candied fruit to raisin mixture; stir well. Add butter mixture and stir until nuts and fruit are thoroughly coated. Drop by heaping tablespoonfuls onto greased baking sheets.

Bake at 375° for 13 minutes or until edges are just beginning to brown. Immediately remove to wire racks to cool. Store in airtight containers between layers of wax paper or freeze up to 1 month. Yield: 7 dozen.

Note: *Cookies become more moist and flavorful the day after preparation.*

Dew Berry's Fruitcake Cookies are divine with a glass of cold eggnog.

Peanut Butter Cup Cookies

My grandmother Ruth would make these cookies around Christmastime when I was little. She'd pull the hot mini-muffin cookies from the oven and urge me to push the peanut butter cups into the centers while still hot. The cookies wouldn't last long—neither would the milk. — *David Gallent*

½ cup sugar
⅓ cup creamy peanut butter
¼ cup butter or margarine, softened
1 large egg
2 tablespoons whipping cream
1 teaspoon vanilla extract
1 cup all-purpose flour
1 teaspoon baking soda
⅛ teaspoon salt
¼ cup chopped unsalted peanuts
1 (13-ounce) package miniature peanut butter cup candies (we tested with Reese's)

Beat first 3 ingredients at medium speed with an electric mixer 2 minutes. Add egg, whipping cream, and vanilla; beat well. Combine flour, soda, and salt. Add to peanut butter mixture; stir well. Stir in peanuts.

Roll dough into ¾" balls. Press dough into miniature (1¾") muffin pans lined with paper cups. Bake at 350° for 12 minutes. Remove from oven; press a peanut butter cup into center of each cookie. Bake 2 more minutes. Remove from oven. Cool completely in pan on a wire rack. Yield: 3½ dozen.

Gretchen's Mocha-Chocolate Chip Biscotti

In college I was given a fabulous basic biscotti recipe. At the time, I was working part-time at a coffeehouse and decided to sell my biscotti to make a little extra money. I developed about fifteen different flavors and began selling to a number of coffeehouses in town. This was one of my bestsellers.
Gretchen Feldtman

- 2 cups all-purpose flour
- 1 teaspoon baking powder
- 1 teaspoon baking soda
- 1/8 teaspoon salt
- 1 cup sugar
- 1/4 cup Swiss-style coffee drink mix (we tested with International Coffee's Suisse Mocha)
- 1 large egg
- 2 egg whites
- 1 teaspoon vanilla extract
- 1 1/2 cups semisweet chocolate mini-morsels, divided
- 2 (2-ounce) vanilla candy coating squares
- 1/2 cup finely chopped chocolate-covered espresso beans

Stir together first 6 ingredients in a large bowl. Combine egg, egg whites, and vanilla; stir until blended. Add egg mixture to flour mixture; stir well (mixture will be very crumbly). Stir in 1/2 cup morsels.

Knead mixture on an unfloured surface. Continue to knead until well blended. Shape into a 14" x 4" log on a lightly greased baking sheet. Bake at 350° for 30 minutes. Remove to a wire rack to cool 10 minutes.

Cut log diagonally into 3/4"-thick slices with a serrated knife, using a gentle sawing motion. Place slices on ungreased baking sheets. Bake 5 minutes; turn cookies over, and bake 5 more minutes. Cool on wire racks.

Microwave candy coating squares in an 11" x 7" baking dish at HIGH 1 minute. Stir in remaining 1 cup morsels. Microwave at HIGH 30 seconds; stir well. Dip 1 long side of each biscotti into chocolate mixture. Sprinkle with espresso beans. Let harden. Yield: 1 1/2 dozen.

Our Five

Favorite Cookie Wraps

Let our cookie-packaging ideas inspire you to get started early on some holiday baking.

1 *Place brownies in a tissue-lined box, such as this monogrammed box. Close box and tie with decorative ribbon. Be sure to enclose a gift card.*

2 *Here's a cute packaging idea for gifts for your child's teachers at school. Stack cookies in cellophane bags; stack bags in tall glasses. Tie each bag with ribbon and add a note saying "serve with milk."*

3 *Empty an oats canister. Wrap canister and lid with white paper, and tape or glue seams. Then wrap the white canister with toile waxed tissue paper, and tape or glue seams. Or forego the white paper and toile tissue, and wrap the canister in holiday wrapping paper. Fill canister with tea cakes, and replace lid. Tie ribbon around canister, and add a gift tag.*

4 *Package cookies or brownies in a tissue-lined corrugated box. Close box, tie with ribbon or jute string, and attach a tag.*

5 *Wrap biscotti in a large piece of cellophane. Tie ends with ribbon, and add a decorative tag.*

Where to Find It

Source information is current at the time of publication, but we cannot guarantee availability of items. If an item is not listed, its source is unknown.

With Southern Style

Contact your favorite florist ahead of time and ask them to order seeded eucalyptus, lavender, heather, or other greenery for holiday decorations.

Pages 8, 12, and 13—mesh cones: SNK Enterprises, P.O. Box 6702, Chesterfield, MO 63006; (314) 991-8570
lanterns: Pottery Barn, (888) 779-5176, www.potterybarn.com
Page 11—twig balls: Michaels Arts and Crafts; (800) 642-4235, www.michaels.com
Page 17—trees: Briarcliff Shop, 2003 Cahaba Road, Birmingham, AL 35223; (205) 870-8110
Page 21—raffia, seed balls, and similar items: Loose Ends, 2065 Madrona Avenue SE, Salem, OR 97302; (503) 390-2348, www.looseends.com
Page 24—crystalline trees: Henhouse Antiques, 1900 Cahaba Road, Birmingham, AL 35223; (205) 918-0505
Page 25—silver reindeer: King's House, 2418 Montevallo Road, Mountain Brook, AL 35223; (205) 871-5787

Tabletop Magic

Pages 30 and 34—candles, placemats, salad plates: Flora, 1911 Oxmoor Road, Homewood, AL 35209; (205) 871-4004;
stemware: Christine's, 2822 Petticoat Lane, Mountain Brook, AL 35223; (205) 871-8297
Pages 31 and 40—pear napkins: Anali, www.anali.com;
red tray: Smith & Hawken, (800) 940-1170, www.smithandhawken.com
Page 33—china, Christmas Rose pattern: Bromberg & Co., (800) 633-4616, www.brombergs.com
Page 35—wreath linens: Anali, www.anali.com
Pages 36–37—china: Bromberg & Co., (800) 633-4616, www.brombergs.com
Page 38—centerpiece bowls: Attic Antiques, 5620 Cahaba Valley Road, Birmingham, AL 35242; (205) 991-6887
Page 39—bowl: Cast Art, 1713 2nd Avenue South, Birmingham, AL 35233; (205) 324-3936;
tablecloth: Christine's, 2822 Petticoat Lane, Mountain Brook, AL 35223; (205) 871-8297;
ribbon: Christmas & Co., P.O. Box 130037, Birmingham, AL 35213; (205) 943-0020, www.christmasandco.com
Page 41—chargers, dinnerware, glassware, candles: Lamb's Ears, 3138 Cahaba Heights Road, Birmingham, AL 35243; (205) 969-3138;
sugar mold: Flora, 1911 Oxmoor Road, Homewood, AL 35209; (205) 871-4004
Page 42—silver container: Pottery Barn, (888) 779-5176, www.potterybarn.com
Page 44—container: *Southern Living At HOME*™, www.southernlivingathome.com for ordering information
Page 45—hat: Smith & Hawken, (800) 940-1170, www.smithandhawken.com
Page 46—plant holder: Global Views, 2600 Perth Street, Dallas, TX 75220; (888) 956-0030, www.globalviews.com
Page 47—container: *Southern Living At HOME*™, www.southernlivingathome.com for ordering information

Casual Holiday Meals

Page 48—props: Attic Antiques, 5620 Cahaba Valley Road, Birmingham, AL 35242; (205) 991-6887
Page 50—china, juice glasses: Bromberg & Co., (800) 633-4616, www.brombergs.com;
silver coffee server: Bridges Antiques, 3949 Cypress Drive, Birmingham, AL 35243; (205) 967-6233;
glass compote: Birmingham Antique Mall, 2211 Magnolia Avenue, Birmingham, AL 35205; (205) 328-7761
Page 54—toile teacups: Neiman Marcus, neimanmarcus.com;
glass punch cups: Birmingham Antique Mall, 2211 Magnolia Avenue, Birmingham, AL 35205; (205) 328-7761;
silver coffee server: Bridges Antiques, 3949 Cypress Drive, Birmingham, AL 35243; (205) 967-6233
Page 55—napkin rings: Christine's, 2822 Petticoat Lane, Mountain Brook, AL 35223; (205) 871-8297
Page 56—quilt, serving pieces, flatware: Attic Antiques, 5620 Cahaba Valley Road, Birmingham, AL 35242; (205) 991-6887;
salt and pepper: Tricia's Treasures, 1433-5 Montgomery Highway, Vestavia Hills, AL 35216; (205) 822-0004;
tree napkin ring/ornament: Flora, 1911 Oxmoor Road, Homewood, AL 35209; (205) 871-4004
Page 57—dinner plates: Barney's New York, 660 Madison Avenue, New York, NY 10021; (212) 826-8900, www.barneys.com;
flatware and glassware: Attic Antiques, 5620 Cahaba Valley Road, Birmingham, AL 35242; (205) 991-6887;
salt and pepper: Tricia's Treasures, 1433-5 Montgomery Hwy, Vestavia Hills, AL 35216; (205) 822-0004

Page 58—jars, gift tags: Attic Antiques, 5620 Cahaba Valley Road, Birmingham, AL 35242; (205) 991-6887
Pages 60–61—props: Attic Antiques, 5620 Cahaba Valley Road, Birmingham, AL 35242; (205) 991-6887
Page 63—pitcher: Catherine's Home Collections, (941) 594-1300; **napkin:** Anali, www.anali.com
Page 64—mugs: Catherine's Home Collections, (941) 594-1300
Page 65—dinner plate: Bromberg & Co., (800) 633-4616, www.brombergs.com
Page 74—all pottery: Pot Luck Studios, 23 Main Street, Accord, NY 12404; (845) 626-2300; www.homeportfolio.com
Page 75—bowl: Eigan Arts Inc., 150 Bay Street, Jersey City, NJ 07302; (201) 798-7310
Pages 78–79—pottery: Pot Luck Studios, 23 Main Street, Accord, NY 12404; (845) 626-2300; www.homeportfolio.com
Pages 83–84—French santons: French Inspirations, (800) 440-1777, and www.ruedefrance.com

There's No Place Like Home

Pages 94 and 125—large candles, glass containers: Flora, 1911 Oxmoor Road, Homewood, AL 35209; (205) 871-4004; **small candles, votive holders:** Pottery Barn, (888) 779-5176, www.potterybarn.com
Pages 95 and 116—twelve days of Christmas ornaments: Midwest® of Cannon Falls, (800) 377-3335, www.midwestofcannonfalls.com
Page 97—toile gift wraps: Two Shabby Chicks, (866) 2SHABBY, www.twoshabbychicks.com; **toile fabric garland:** Midwest® of Cannon Falls, (800) 377-3335, www.midwestofcannonfalls.com; **toile napkins and plates:** Caspari, 116 East 27th Street, New York, NY 10016; (800) 227-7274
Page 98—two-handled jarron: Catherine's Home Collections, (941) 594-1300
Page 102—J-O-Y letters: Flora, 1911 Oxmoor Road, Homewood, AL 35209; (205) 871-4004
Page 103—star votive holders, reindeer: Christmas & Co., P.O. Box 130037, Birmingham, AL 35213; (205) 943-0020, www.christmasandco.com
Page 105—reindeer and sleigh: King's House, 2418 Montevallo Road, Mountain Brook, AL 35223; (205) 871-5787
Pages 108–109—candleholders: Cast Art, 1713 2nd Avenue South, Birmingham, AL 35233; (205) 324-3936

Page 111—snowmen: Midwest® of Cannon Falls, (800) 377-3335, www.midwestofcannonfalls.com; Christmas & Co., P.O. Box 130037, Birmingham, AL 35213; (205) 943-0020, www.christmasandco.com; and Attic Antiques, 5620 Cahaba Valley Road, Birmingham, AL 35242; (205) 991-6887
Pages 113–115—containers: *Southern Living At HOME™*, www.southernlivingathome.com for ordering information
Page 118—ornaments: Christmas & Co., P.O. Box 130037, Birmingham, AL 35213; (205) 943-0020, www.christmasandco.com
Page 119—pressed-tin cones: Midwest® of Cannon Falls, (800) 377-3335, www.midwestofcannonfalls.com
Page 120—oversize balls and cones: Midwest® of Cannon Falls, (800) 377-3335, www.midwestofcannonfalls.com
Page 121—snowflake ornaments: Midwest® of Cannon Falls, (800) 377-3335, www.midwestofcannonfalls.com and Lamb's Ears, 3138 Cahaba Heights Road, Birmingham, AL 35243; (205) 969-3138
Page 122—candles, glass urns, beaded wreaths: Pottery Barn, (888) 779-5176, www.potterybarn.com
Page 123—angel candleholder: Flora, 1911 Oxmoor Road, Homewood, AL 35209; (205) 871-4004; **votive holders:** Midwest® of Cannon Falls, (800) 377-3335, www.midwestofcannonfalls.com; **candle:** Pottery Barn, (888) 779-5176, www.potterybarn.com
Page 124—chandelier: Lamb's Ears, 3138 Cahaba Heights Road, Birmingham, AL 35243; (205) 969-3138
Page 125—bobeches and candles: Lamb's Ears, 3138 Cahaba Heights Road, Birmingham, AL 35243; (205) 969-3138

It's the Thought

Pages 126 and 134—faux acorns: David's Flowers, (770) 395-7638
Page 135—thin colored foam: Michaels Arts and Crafts, (800) 642-4235, www.michaels.com

Holiday Recipes

Page 146—dinner plate: *Southern Living At HOME™*, www.southernlivingathome.com for ordering information
Page 148—bowl: *Southern Living At HOME™*, www.southernlivingathome.com for ordering information
Page 159—unbleached all-purpose flour: King Arthur Flour, www.kingarthurflour.com
Pages 168–169—monogrammed box, toile waxed tissue paper: Williams-Sonoma, www.williams-sonoma.com
Back cover—toile Santa: Christine's, 2822 Petticoat Lane, Mountain Brook, AL 35223; (205) 871-8297

Patterns & Instructions

Splendidly Styled *(pages 96-97)*

To make the bottle bag, cut fabric to the desired size. Fold the fabric in half, with right sides facing and raw edges aligned. Glue or stitch along the side and bottom edges. Allow glue to dry, and carefully turn bag right side out. Fold down the excess fabric at the top of the bag, and tuck in around the bottle. Tie ribbon or raffia around the neck of the bottle. Personalize the ribbon using a fabric paint pen, if desired.

"Hand"some Tags

(page 135)

Enlarge or reduce pattern on photocopier to desired size.

Punch hole here.

Tag Pattern

Sweet Containers *(page 128)*

Enlarge or reduce pattern on photocopier to desired size.

Punch hole here.

Cone Pattern

Punch hole here.

General Index

Birdhouses, 107
blue-and-white, 106
bottle bags, 96
bows
how-to, 10
ribbon loops, 14

Candles, 94, 103, 108–109, 113, 115, 122–125
floating, 94, 125
centerpieces, 30–31, 34–35, 38–43
chandelier decorations, 20, 43, 118–119, 124
Christmas trees, 16, 21
collections, 106–111
cones
mesh, 8, 12–13
ornaments, 119–120
paper, 128–131
copper, 110

Dried materials, 21

Evergreen charger, 33

Fabric plates, 99
floral decorations, 8, 12–13, 18, 20–24, 35, 42–47, 103–104, 114–115, 119
poinsettias, 26, 42–43, 46
front doors, 10–13, 100
fabric-wrapped, 100
fruit decorations, 38–41, 102, 113–115
apples, 29, 38
pears, 31, 40–41

Garlands, 8, 10–13, 17–19, 22–26, 28–29, 32, 116–117, 120
gifts
for pets, 133
plants, 44–45, 47
wrappings, 97, 126–137
bottle bags, 96
container ideas, 135
food gifts, 97, 128–129
naturals, 126, 134, 136–137
package topper ideas, 136–137
tags, 135–136

Lanterns, 12–13

Mantel decorations, 17–18, 22–23, 29, 106–107, 116–117

Nails, in masonry, 10
napkin
folds, 36–37
ties, 34
nuts, 115

Ornaments, 95, 116–121

Pinecones, 112, 115
wiring, 10

Ribbon loops, 14

Silver decorations, 22–25, 35, 42, 102–105
tips, 105
snowmen, 111

Tablescapes, 9, 19–20, 24–25, 27, 30–35, 43, 46, 94
table topper, no-sew, 98
toile-themed decorations, 96–101
topiaries
carnation, 115
ivy, 19, 24, 43–44
outdoor, 101
rosemary, 9, 20, 27, 29
tree topper, 21

Vases, 112–115

Wreaths
evergreen, 14–15, 26, 29, 100
magnolia, 12–13

Recipe Index

Almonds
- Sausage and Wild Rice Casserole, 52
- Shortbread, Almond, 160
- Thumbprints, Raspberry-Almond, 164

Appetizers
- Crab Cakes with Red Pepper Mayonnaise, Prosciutto, 73
- Dip, Florentine Artichoke, 141
- Green Olive Relish, 70
- Kalamata Olive Relish, 70
- Roasted Onions, Figs, and Smoked Sausage, 70
- Toasted Pita Wedges, 70
- Walnut-Basil Pastries with Dried Tomatoes, 72

Apples
- Baked Apples, Sausage and Pecan, 153
- Candied Sweet Potatoes and Apples, 59
- Pie, Cornmeal Streusel Apple, 79

Beans
- Chili, Thick Three-Bean, 62
- Green Bean Casserole with Fried Leeks, 78
- Green Beans, Homestyle, 59
- Green Beans with Basil and Orange, French, 87

Beef Brisket with Shiitake Mushrooms and Red Wine Sauce, 147

Beverages
- Punch, Hot Percolator, 55
- Wine, Hot Spiced, 62

Breads
- Biscuits, Cheese, 55
- Pita Wedges, Toasted, 70
- Scones, Cheddar, 64

Cakes
- Bûche de Noël, Mocha-Orange, 88
- Coffee Cake, Banana Streusel, 55
- Fudge Cake, New Orleans Double-Chocolate Christmas Praline-, 144
- Pound Cake with Fresh Orange Syrup, Orange, 61

Casseroles
- Chicken-and-Wild Rice Casserole, Leslie's Favorite, 142
- Sausage and Wild Rice Casserole, 52

Cheese
- Biscuits, Cheese, 55
- Cheddar Scones, 64
- Cream Cheese Scrambled Eggs, 52
- Pastries with Dried Tomatoes, Walnut-Basil, 72
- Potatoes, Scalloped, 87
- Ricotta Spread, Walnut-, 72
- Roquefort, and Caramelized Onion Galette, Pear, 156

Chicken
- Casserole, Leslie's Favorite Chicken-and-Wild Rice, 142
- Fricassee, Chicken, 149

Chili
- con Carne, Chipotle Chili, 148
- Three-Bean Chili, Thick, 62

Chocolate
- Biscotti, Gretchen's Mocha-Chocolate Chip, 168
- Brownies, Fudgy Peppermint Candy, 167
- Bûche de Noël, Mocha-Orange, 88
- Cake, New Orleans Double-Chocolate Christmas Praline-Fudge, 144
- Cookies, Easy Oatmeal-Chocolate Chip, 163
- Cookies, Triple-Nut Chocolate Clover, 166
- Cookies, White Chocolate, Peanut, and Caramel Candy, 155
- Crackles, Spicy Chocolate, 64
- Fudgy Mocha Melt, 93
- Ganache, Chocolate, 144
- Pie, Bourbon-Chocolate Pecan, 143
- Shortbread, Cookies 'n' Cream, 159
- Shortbread, Peanut Butter-Chocolate Chip, 161
- Tart, Chocolate-Peanut, 155

Condiments
- Cream, Mock Devonshire, 53
- Mayonnaise, Red Pepper, 73

Cookies. *See also* Shortbread.
- Biscotti, Gretchen's Mocha-Chocolate Chip, 168
- Brownies, Fudgy Peppermint Candy, 167
- Chocolate Crackles, Spicy, 64
- Fruitcake Cookies, Dew Berry's, 165
- Oatmeal-Chocolate Chip Cookies, Easy, 163
- Peanut Butter Cup Cookies, 165
- Shortbread Crisps, Pistachio, 67
- Tea Cakes, Aunt Neal's Old-Fashioned, 164
- Thumbprints, Raspberry-Almond, 164
- Triple-Nut Chocolate Clover Cookies, 166
- White Chocolate, Peanut, and Caramel Candy Cookies, 155

Desserts
- Custards with Crunchy Pecan Topping, Pumpkin, 156
- Fudgy Mocha Melt, 93
- Vanilla-Coconut Pears, 91

Eggs, Cream Cheese Scrambled, 52

Fish and Shellfish
- Crab Cakes with Red Pepper Mayonnaise, Prosciutto, 73
- Oyster and Pear Salad, Fried, 84
- Shrimp and Sweet Potato Gumbo, 91
- Seafood Gumbo, 149

Fruitcake Cookies, Dew Berry's, 165

Goose with Currant Sauce, Roast, 85

Ham
Brown Sugar Honey-Crusted Ham, 58
Croutons, Sweet Potato-Peanut Soup with Ham, 151
Prosciutto Crab Cakes with Red Pepper Mayonnaise, 73

Nuts. *See also* specific types.
Pistachio Shortbread Crisps, 67
Triple-Nut Chocolate Clover Cookies, 166
Walnut-Ricotta Spread, 72

Onion
Galette, Pear, Roquefort, and Caramelized Onion, 156
Roasted Onions, Figs, and Smoked Sausage, 70
Orange
Bûche de Noël, Mocha-Orange, 88
Pound Cake with Fresh Orange Syrup, Orange, 61
Dressing, Rice and Pecan Salad with Orange-Thyme, 151
Green Beans with Basil and Orange, French, 87
Syrup, Fresh Orange, 61

Pasta
Manicotti, Shiitake Mushroom and Spinach, 67
Peanuts
Chews, Salted Peanut, 166
Cookies, Peanut Butter Cup, 165
Cookies, White Chocolate, Peanut, and Caramel Candy, 155
Snack Mix, Nutty, 152
Soup with Ham Croutons, Sweet Potato-Peanut, 151
Tart, Chocolate-Peanut, 155
Pears
Galette, Pear, Roquefort, and Caramelized Onion, 156
Ruby Pears, 52
Salad, Fried Oyster and Pear, 84
Vanilla-Coconut Pears, 91
Pecans
Apples, Sausage and Pecan Baked, 153
Cookies, Dew Berry's Fruitcake, 165
Cookies, Easy Oatmeal-Chocolate Chip, 163
Frosting, Praline, 144
Pie, Bourbon-Chocolate Pecan, 143
Salad with Orange-Thyme Dressing, Rice and Pecan, 151
Snack Mix, Nutty, 152
Topping, Pumpkin Custards with Crunchy Pecan, 156
Pies and Pastries
Apple Pie, Cornmeal Streusel, 79
Chocolate-Peanut Tart, 155
Pecan Pie, Bourbon-Chocolate, 143
Walnut-Basil Pastries with Dried Tomatoes, 72
Pork. *See also* Ham and Sausage.
Roast and Browned Potatoes, Mustard-Crusted Pork, 77
Tenderloin, Fruit-Stuffed Pork, 148
Potatoes. *See also* Sweet Potatoes.
Browned Potatoes, Mustard-Crusted Pork Roast and, 77
Scalloped Potatoes, 87

Relishes
Corn Relish, Country, 58
Olive Relish, Green, 70
Olive Relish, Kalamata, 70

Salad Dressings
Orange-Thyme Dressing, Rice and Pecan Salad with, 151
Tangerine Dressing, 66
Salads
Field Greens with Tangerine Dressing and Pesto Wafers, 66
Fried Oyster and Pear Salad, 84
Rice and Pecan Salad with Orange-Thyme Dressing, 151
Sweet Potato Salad, Roasted, 141
Sauces
Cranapple Sauce, Cinnamon-Scented, 77
Currant Sauce, 85
Sausage
Apples, Sausage and Pecan Baked, 153
Casserole, Sausage and Wild Rice, 52
Smoked Sausage, Roasted Onions, Figs, and, 70
Shortbread
Almond Shortbread, 160
Basic Shortbread, 159
Coffee-Toffee Shortbread, Chewy, 160
Cookies 'n' Cream Shortbread, 159
Peanut Butter-Chocolate Chip Shortbread, 161
Peanut Butter Shortbread, 161
Pistachio Shortbread Crisps, 67
Slow Cooker
Beef Brisket with Shiitake Mushrooms and Red Wine Sauce, 147
Chicken Fricassee, 149
Chili con Carne, Chipotle, 148
Pork Tenderloin, Fruit-Stuffed, 148
Turkey and Dressing, Slow Cooker, 147
Soups
Butternut Squash Soup, 76
Sweet Potato-Peanut Soup with Ham Croutons, 151
Spinach
Dip, Florentine Artichoke, 141
Manicotti, Shiitake Mushroom and Spinach, 67
Sweet Potatoes
Candied Sweet Potatoes and Apples, 59
Gumbo, Shrimp and Sweet Potato, 91
Salad, Roasted Sweet Potato, 141
Soup with Ham Croutons, Sweet Potato-Peanut, 151

Turkey
Pot Pie, Green Chile-Turkey, 93
Slow Cooker Turkey and Dressing, 147

Vegetables. *See also* specific types.
Cabbage, Sautéed Red, 87
Corn Relish, Country, 58
Tomatoes with Cilantro, Lime-Marinated, 93

Contributors

Editorial Contributors

Margaret Agnew
Rebekah and Abigail Crowe
Adrienne Short Davis
Alicia Frazier
Kelley Gage
Jan Hanby
Susan Huff
Alisa Hyde
Laurie Knowles
Elizabeth Taliaferro

Thanks to the Following Homeowners

Barbara and Leon Ashford
Gina and Buddy Cox
Jill and Mike Crowe
Dale Fritz
Penny and Mike Fuller
Kelley and Pete Gage
Peggy Goodwin
Carolyn and John Hartman
Joy and Price Kloess
Barbara and Ed Randle
Sally Ratliff
Alice and Robert Schleusner
Sallie and Joe Sherrill
Janie and Allan Trippe
Linda and Kneeland Wright

Thanks to the Following Businesses and Organizations

Attic Antiques
Birmingham Antique Mall
Briarcliff Shop
Briarwood Presbyterian Church
Bridges Antiques
Bromberg & Company
Cast Art
Christine's
Christmas & Co.
Flora
Harmony Landing
Henhouse Antiques
Lamb's Ears
Midwest® of Cannon Falls
Seibels Catalog & Company Store
Tricia's Treasures

Holiday Planning Guide

Get a head start on holiday plans with the help of this handy guide. Use the spacious calendars to keep track of special events, note your menu ideas and holiday errands in the list boxes, and find dozens of useful tips throughout. With this special section, it's easy to be prepared for all the fun the season has to offer.

November Planning Calendar . .178

December Planning Calendar . .180

Helpful Holiday Hints 182

Entertaining Planner 184

Christmas Dinner Planner 186

Gifts & Greetings 188

Holiday Memories 190

Notes & Ideas For Next Year . . .192

NOVEMBER

Sunday	Monday	Tuesday	Wednesday
3	4	5	6
10	11	12	13
17	18	19	20
24	25	26	27

2002

Fill in the calendar spaces with all the activities you have planned for this month. You'll be organized and ready for anything!

Thursday	Friday	Saturday
	1	2
7	8	9
14	15	16
21	22	23
Thanksgiving 28	29	30

THINGS TO DO:

DECEMBER

Sunday	Monday	Tuesday	Wednesday
1	2	3	4
8	9	10	11
15	16	17	18
22	23	Christmas Eve 24	Christmas 25
29	30	New Year's Eve 31	

2002

All will be merry and bright when you start this busy month with a good game plan. Noting important dates on this calendar will help you fit in all the events you love best.

Thursday	Friday	Saturday
5	6	7
12	13	14
19	20	21
26	27	28

THINGS TO DO:

Helpful Holiday Hints

Breeze through the holidays with these expert cooking and decorating tips from our editors.

Fast & Festive Decorating

•Showcase ornaments in a glass bowl for an easy, no-maintenance centerpiece.

•Gather miscellaneous dishes from around your house, fill them with jelly beans or chocolate candies, and tuck a handwritten note in each dish with one word of holiday cheer (such as "Rejoice!").

•Place several clove-spiked oranges in a bright bowl in your kitchen to create a refreshing holiday scent.

•Gather backyard evergreen cuttings to use anywhere holiday spirit is needed. Allow cut stems to soak in water overnight before arranging. Display in vases and accent with pinecones, berries, and fresh fruit.

Christmas Cleanup Tips

•While entertaining for the holidays, keep a disaster kit handy. To deal with the inevitable spills, have paper towels, a couple of small plastic trash bags, and club soda stashed strategically. A splash of club soda followed by a quick blotting with a paper towel will often prevent a small spill from becoming a major stain.

•Opening presents is a joyous family activity, but it can produce a generous pile of boxes, tissue paper, and gift wrap. To make short work of taming the mess, have a couple of large trash bags handy. Resist the temptation to burn wrapping paper in the fireplace; the colored inks can release toxic fumes when burned, and smoldering paper can blow out of the chimney, creating a fire hazard.

Silver Shortcuts

•When serving food in silver pieces, use a glass bowl or liner to prevent acidic foods (such as tomatoes, citrus fruit, and mayonnaise) from coming in contact with silver. Also, salt will pit silver.

•Do not scrape wax off a silver candlestick with a sharp object; you may damage the finish. Instead, place the candlestick in the freezer to harden wax, and then gently chip it off with your fingernail.

•Polishing mitts and cloths designed specifically for silver care are convenient for removing light tarnish. Polishing mitts, cloths, and tarnish strips usually can be found where silver polish is sold and at large housewares stores.

•Old toothbrushes and paper towels are not good substitutes for polishing cloths because they might mar the finish.

•Store silver with tarnish-preventative silver strips. Placing silver in a sealed zip-top plastic bag should give you about six months of tarnish protection.

•When silver is deeply tarnished, resist the urge to try a "miracle dip." Silver dips will remove the tarnish, but they often take off the finish and give the piece a greenish-yellow appearance. Take heavily tarnished pieces to a reputable jewelry or silver shop for a professional cleaning. Remember, a deep tarnish in crevices on ornate silver actually adds character!

•Use your silver! The pieces only get better with use.

Party Essentials

Organize a party closet filled with all the items you'll need for holiday activities. With a well-stocked closet, you'll be set for a season of easy entertaining.

•Centerpieces. Have at least one pretty container, such as a tureen or trifle dish, for the base of your centerpiece. In a pinch, a glass trifle dish filled with fruit makes an easy, last-minute centerpiece.

•Fabric and ribbons. Purchase a few yards of fabrics in holiday hues to swirl loosely down the center of the table. There's no need to hem the edges; just turn them under. Use coordinating ribbons to tie up napkins and flatware for easy handling.

•Votive candleholders. Collect these by the dozen, and you'll have enough to spread a Christmassy glow all through the house: on the dining table, along the mantel, and in the guest bath.

•Serving pieces. For casual entertaining, use baskets for easy cleanup. Select colorful holiday napkins or tea towels to use as basket liners. Large bowls make entertaining easy because you don't have to refill them very often. White serving pieces are good choices; they complement various food items and coordinate well with predominantly white dinner plates.

•For beverages. You'll need an ice bucket and tongs. Wine carafes make attractive serving pitchers. A large coffeepot makes it easy to accommodate a group. Consider purchasing a pot jointly with a neighbor; then you can take turns using it.

Microwave Shortcuts

Melting butter or margarine

Place butter in a microwave-safe glass measure; microwave at HIGH until melted.

1 to 2 tablespoons	20 to 30 seconds
1/4 to 1/2 cup	40 to 50 seconds
3/4 cup	50 to 60 seconds
1 cup	1 to 1 1/2 minutes

Softening butter or margarine

Place butter in a microwave-safe measure or on a plate; microwave at LOW (10% power) until softened.

1 to 2 tablespoons	10 to 30 seconds
1/4 to 1/2 cup	30 seconds to 1 minute
1 cup	1 to 1 1/2 minutes

Note: Time ranges are given for 750-watt and 1,000-watt ovens, starting with cold butter or margarine. When using margarine (which melts quicker than butter) and when using a higher watt oven, check at the lower time range.

Make It . . . Quick & Easy

•Use a pizza cutter to cut dough or to cut day-old bread into cubes for croutons—it's faster than a knife.

•To make cracker crumbs or cookie crumbs without a food processor, place crackers or cookies in a heavy-duty, zip-top plastic bag; roll with a rolling pin or pound with a meat mallet.

White Christmas

Group a variety of white, blooming plants or cut flowers for a dramatic wintry display. Choose several shapes and sizes. There are many possibilities to choose from, such as poinsettias, paperwhites, crocus, and baby's breath. Unify the grouping by using similar containers throughout.

Entertaining Planner

Good planning pays off with great parties. Use these pages to help make this holiday's events fun and memorable.

Guest List

Use these lines to list names and phone numbers of guests you plan to invite to your holiday festivities.

Menu

Check out the recipe index on page 174 for kitchen-tested menus that are already planned for you.

Pantry List

Take a quick inventory of your supplies, and jot down needed items on these lines.

Party To-Do List

Planning ahead is half the task. Make notes here to ensure that nothing is forgotten.

Last-Minute Details

You won't sweat the small stuff when you've written it down beforehand.

Buffet Planner

A week or more before the party:

- Buy all staples and ingredients for dishes to be made ahead.
- Buy or freeze plenty of ice cubes.
- Plan the buffet table centerpieces, if using any.
- Check all linens.

A few days before the party:

- Do major housecleaning.

The day before the party:

- Wash plates and glasses.
- Set up the buffet table and beverage service.

On the party day:

- Complete all final food preparations.
- Give the house a light cleaning.
- Clear a space for your guests to leave coats.

Christmas Dinner Planner

Start early with your plans so you can turn this year's traditional dinner into something extra special.

Guest List

On these lines, write the names and phone numbers of guests you plan to invite to your holiday dinner.

Menu

Add a taste of the South to this year's meal with our Country Christmas menu on page 56.

Dinner To-Do List

This list can include everything from buying the food to setting the table.

Christmas Dinner Stress-Savers

•This time of year, refrigerator storage space is at a premium, so start a new holiday ritual: A weekly refrigerator cleaning. Designate a day (the day before trash pickup is a good one) to reclaim refrigerator space from old leftovers and expired items and make room for special seasonal dishes.

•Plan ahead. Have the table set, flowers arranged, and anything non-food-related done the day before so you can devote your time to enjoying the food, family, and guests during the celebration.

•Designate an area for beverages. This will allow guests to serve themselves, creating an opportunity for them to make themselves at home and freeing you to tend to other duties.

•Identify serving pieces and utensils for each dish ahead of time. Place a slip of paper with the name of the recipe to be served on each piece. You'll save yourself from that last-minute rush to find your favorite serving platter.

•Prepare as many recipes ahead of time as possible. Write out the baking or reheating instructions and tape them to the cover of the dish. Not only will this reduce the stress of last minute food-preparation, but it will also eliminate cookbook clutter and the mountain of pots and pans in the sink when guests arrive.

•Clean up as you go. Start the party with an empty trash can and an empty dishwasher, and wash pots and pans as you use them.

Kitchen Time-Cutters

Measure dry ingredients before moist ones to minimize cleanup. Before measuring honey and other sticky ingredients, rinse the measure with hot water; then the honey will slide right out.

Chop dry ingredients such as breadcrumbs or nuts in a food processor first. Then chop or shred moist or wet foods without washing the workbowl.

Use a food processor to chop, slice, or shred several ingredients consecutively or together without washing the workbowl if the ingredients will be combined later.

Chop and freeze ½-cup portions of green pepper, onion, and parsley in zip-top freezer bags, or purchase prepackaged frozen chopped onions and green pepper. When you have extra time, prepare dry breadcrumbs, shredded cheese, and toasted nuts to freeze.

Buy ingredients in closest-to-usable form. Choose items such as skinned and boned chicken breasts, peeled shrimp, and shredded cheese. Select bags of precut produce at your supermarket, or purchase ready-made ingredients at the salad bar.

When slicing vegetables such as carrots, green onions, or celery, slice 3 or 4 pieces at a time.

Cut vegetables into small pieces or thin slices to cook faster.

Substitute an equal amount of ready-to-serve chicken broth for homemade chicken stock.

Holiday Touches for the Table

•Write guests' names and the date on plain ornaments using a paint pen. Use the personalized ornaments as place cards and party favors.

•Stack small, wrapped packages containing party favors on a cake stand, or scatter them across the tabletop. After the meal, guests can choose a gift from the assortment for a take-home treasure.

•Tuck napkins and flatware into colorful mittens. The pairs of mittens double as place favors.

Gifts & Greetings

Give your memory a break, and keep a current list of gifts and greetings (both sent and received) on these pages. You'll be so glad you did—especially next year!

Christmas Card List

Name	Address	Sent/Received

Gift List

Name	Gift	Sent/Delivered

Create a Gift-Wrapping Station

•Set up a card table in an out-of-the-way corner of your home to create a wrapping center. Try to keep the surface free of decorations and food.

•In addition to wrapping paper, gift tags, bows, and ribbons, stock the area with extra scissors and tape designated for wrapping use only. Also, don't forget pens or markers for writing on gift tags. (To prevent ink smears on shiny tag surfaces, use a fine-point permanent marker, such as Sharpie®.)

•Clean, kitchen-size trash cans are great for holding rolls of gift wrap, and the vertical storage uses minimal space. Keep rubber bands handy to slide on wrapping paper tubes to prevent paper from unrolling and rumpling. After the holiday rush is over, take advantage of post-holiday markdowns and stock up on gift wrap. Store it in the "gift-wrap can" for next Christmas.

HOLIDAY MEMORIES

Savor every moment of this season's celebrations by recording them on these pages.

TREASURED TRADITIONS

Traditions are key ingredients of Christmas festivities. Write some of your favorite ones on the lines below.

SPECIAL HOLIDAY EVENTS

Yuletide happenings provide wonderful memories. Here's a place to list this year's best.

Holiday Visits & Visitors

Use this space to write fun anecdotes about holiday gatherings. It's also a good place to write a reminder to yourself of people you especially want to visit during the holidays.

Favorite Holiday Recipes

Appetizers and Beverages:

Entrées:

Sides and Salads:

Cookies and Candies:

Desserts:

Notes & Ideas for Next Year

Things We Loved

Make a note here of this year's tastiest recipes, best decorating ideas, and overall favorites so you can have a repeat performance next year.

Works In Progress

See any good ideas this season that you'd like to try yourself? Record them here so you can include them in your plans for Christmas 2003!

Party Ideas	Decorations	Recipes

New Year's Resolutions